Law, Antisemitism and the Holocaust

Whilst an increasing amount of attention is being paid to law's connection or involvement with National Socialism, less attention is focused upon thinking through the links between law and the emergence of antisemitism. As a consequence, antisemitism is presented as a pre-existent given, as something that is the object, rather than the subject of study. In this way, the question of law's connection to antisemitism is presented as one of external application. In this ironic mimesis of the positivist tradition, the question of a potentially more intimate or dialectical connection between law and antisemitism is avoided.

This work differs from these accounts by explaining the relationship between law and antisemitism through a discussion of these issues by critical thinkers from the mid-nineteenth century to the present – that is, from Marx to Agamben through Nietzsche, Sartre, Adorno and Horkheimer, Arendt and Lyotard. Despite the differences that exists between each thinker, one particular common critical theme unites them. That theme is the connections they make, in diverse ways, between legal rights as an expression of modern political emancipation and the emergence and development of the social phenomenon of antisemitism.

Approaching the question of the relationship between law and antisemitism in this way not only brings into question the popular, but ultimately mistaken, notion of an 'eternal antisemitism', but brings into doubt the idea of a monolithic 'modern' antisemitism, that emerges fully formed, unchanging and static. The thinkers discussed in this work are examined not only for their insights and accounts of the development of antisemitism, but also as expressions of the particular societies in which they were writing. In this way, a further aim of the project comes into focus, that of the impact of the Holocaust upon critical forms of thought itself.

David M. Seymour is a lecturer at Lancaster University Law School. His key research interests are law, antisemitism and the Holocaust; law and aesthetics; contemporary social and legal theory.

Law, Antisemitism and the Holocaust

David M. Seymour

Routledge
Taylor & Francis Group
LONDON AND NEW YORK
a Glass House book

First published 2007
by Routledge
2 Park Square, Milton Park, Abingdon, Oxon OX14 4RN

Simultaneously published in the USA and Canada
by Routledge
711 Third Avenue, New York, NY 10017, USA

*Routledge is an imprint of the Taylor & Francis Group,
an informa business*

A GlassHouse book

© 2007 Seymour, David

Typeset in Times by
RefineCatch Limited, Bungay, Suffolk

All rights reserved. No part of this book may be reprinted or reproduced or utilised in any form or by any electronic, mechanical, or other means, now known or hereafter invented, including photocopying and recording, or in any information storage or retrieval system, without permission in writing from the publishers.

British Library Cataloguing in Publication Data
A catalogue record for this book is available from the British Library

Library of Congress Cataloging-in-Publication Data
Seymour, David (David M.)
Law, antisemitism and the holocaust / by David Seymour.
    p.   cm.
Includes bibliographical references.
ISBN-13: 978–0–415–42040–2 (pbk.)
ISBN-10: 0–415–42040–7 (pbk.)
ISBN-13: 978–1–904385–43–1 (hardback)
ISBN-10: 1–904385–43–5 (hardback)
[etc.]
   1. Jews—Legal status, laws, etc.—Europe.   2. Antisemitism—Europe.   3. Holocaust, Jewish (1939–1945).   I. Title.
KJC5144.M56.S48 2007
323.1192′.404—dc22
                                                            2007026053

ISBN-13: 978–0–415–42040–2 (pbk)
ISBN-10: 0–415–42040–7 (pbk)

ISBN-13: 978–1–904385–43–1 (hbk)
ISBN-10: 1–904385–43–5 (hbk)

eISBN-13: 978–0–203–93844–7
eISBN-10: 0–203–93844–5

To, and for, Alison

Contents

	Preface	ix
	Introduction	xvii
1	Karl Marx: dissolving the Jewish question	1
2	From critique to positivism: domination and the naturalisation of antisemitism	13
3	The absence of contradiction and the contradiction of absence: law, ethics and the Holocaust	33
4	Antisemitism and emancipation: the *ressentiment* of loss	49
5	The slave, the noble and the Jew: reflections on section 7 of *On the Genealogy of Morals*	83
6	The jurisprudence of Nazi monumental architecture	97
7	Conclusion: Hannah Arendt – the genealogy of antisemitism	113
	Bibliography	127
	Index	135

Acknowledgements

I should like to acknowledge the patience and constant support of Beverly Brown and Colin Perrin at Routledge-Cavendish, and of copy editor, Elizabeth McElwain. For a variety of reasons, all of which connected with this book, I would like to thank Gillian Rose, Annie Phizaclea, Jane Tyrell, Peter Wagner, Howard Caygill, Barry Collins, Qudsia Mirza, Peter Rowe, Sol Picciotto, Geraint Howells, Steven Riley, Marty Lyons, Bill MacNeil, David Hirsh, Didi Herman, Richard Seymour, Joe Seymour, Mildred Seymour, Stuart Abrahams, Anne Abrahams, Alan Diduck, Marlene Lagimodiere, Agata Fijalkowski and Max Seymour. My immense gratitude goes to Robert Fine whose personal and professional commitment to this work exceeded all reasonable – and unreasonable – expectations. And, in keeping with the quiet dignity of the understated, thanks to Alison Diduck.

Preface
Letter from Venice

Venice, 1597
My dear friend,

The little news that reaches me here is resplendent with tales of love. Love, how that little word sticks in my throat! I am told that at Belmont, the palace of that fair and gentle Portia, love reigns supreme; such perfect and ideal love. The love of husband and wife, Portia and Bassanio, Lorenzo, and, oh, how that pains me, my daughter Jessica, and the love of friends, Antonio and Bassanio. How they must spend their days in idyllic bliss, without a care in the world. And yet, my dear friend, only I know what all these lovers and friends know themselves but do not dare acknowledge – that love has a price, that love has a cost. And who has paid for their love? Me, Shylock, the one who was once known as Shylock the Jew. And how have I paid? With my money, my religion, and my future. Without exaggeration, I could even say that I have paid for their love, their happiness, with my own life.

And how did this bitter-sweet tale come to pass? This I shall tell you, and in so telling leave out nothing – nothing – including the part I myself played in my own downfall and in their victory.

A few months ago, the noble Bassanio came to visit me. He requested three thousand ducats. Why he wanted them at the time I did not know. It later came to my knowledge that he needed them so as to have the means to court the woman of his heart, Portia. He needed my money for his love! For his happiness! Yet, do you hear a word about this part of the story, about how I furnished him with the money so that he was free to love? About how Jewish money paved the way for that most perfect of loves? Oh, how much more I shall tell you of this association of Jewish money and Christian love.

Needless to say Bassanio, who knows how to spend money, but not how to produce it, was not in a position to make any kind of deal with me. I have since heard it told that Antonio the merchant, of whom I shall tell you a great deal more, had already given him – given, do you note, not lent, but given, and given out of friendship, out of love! – had given Bassanio a great deal of money so that he could invest in ventures. Apparently, he had asked Antonio to give him more, but Antonio was unable to.

But, and here lies the first of many infamies, do you know what justification Bassanio, this paragon of virtue, gave to Antonio in requesting yet more of his friend's money? I shall tell you. He pleaded his request by arguing that since Portia had been bequeathed a great fortune, and since whoever won her would gain control of that wealth, both the later gift and the earlier one would be repaid a hundred fold. So much for the purity of love! These Christians, these merchants, they treat the affairs of the heart as if it were a business deal. Yet, it is the Jew that bears the weight of that assumption!

Be that as it may, Antonio was not in a position to give his friend the funds he needed so as to satisfy his heart's desire. His money was idle, tied up in goods sitting on ships in the middle of the ocean. The two were left, despite themselves, to come to me. To ask *me* for the money, to ask *me* to furnish the cost of Bassanio's love.

When they came to see me, Bassanio did not mention even a word in my presence about his love, nor about the potential return that such love was to furnish. I suppose that they thought that love was an alien notion to me. What little they know! I know only too well about love, but I keep it in its place. Unlike those noble compatriots, Bassanio and Antonio, who speak of love in the same breath as profit, I keep the two firmly separated. Love is for the heart, money for the pocket.

Bassanio, perhaps because of the intensity of his feelings, his need to stand a chance to win his heart's prize, was pleasant enough toward me in asking me to lend him the sum. True, I heard in his voice his hatred with which he treats a Jew, but, what's the news in that! As I have said, I do not lend out of love, but out of calculation. But my calculating mind knew that his coffers were empty. On his own, I would have refused him without a second thought. But, and such a small word for such a great consequence, he then assured me that Antonio would stand surety.

Antonio, Antonio. Oh, how long I had waited to catch him on the hip. He was not like the other Christians that I have dealt with, either as friend or client. He hated me, but he hated me in a novel and original way. He is unlike those Christians who hated me for their usual reasons, killing their Lord, and for refusing the truth of the 'one true religion', etc., etc. That is their only reason for despising me, even while they knew that I was necessary for them.

I was necessary to give them money to live, since in the way they lived, they could make none of their own; they used money to consume – no more, no less. Apparently, it goes against their Church for them to make money make money. Even in their hatred of me and my people, we remained a part of their lives and their world. But not so to Antonio and his new breed of merchants.

Antonio and his kind believe that they have found a way around their Church's prohibitions. Instead of money making money through interest, money makes money for them through profit. A fine distinction! Tell me my dear friend, what is the difference between buying cheap and selling dear, and charging interest on money lent? Is it not true that in both ways the recipient gives back more to the provider than the provider has laid out? Ah, you might say, but the man who provides the goods still needs us Jews to give those who buy the money to purchase what is supplied them in this way. That is not the case. And why is that not the case? I shall tell you.

The merchant faces those who come into contact with him in two ways – as a buyer and as a seller. First, he buys what they have made with his own money; then he takes those goods and exchanges them with others that a another merchant has acquired in the same way, and – this part is so clever that I do not know why a Jew did not think of it – he sells those goods back to the same people who made them originally, but this time for a far greater price. In this way, money constantly reproduces itself through the work of people who make things themselves, but who then buy those things back as if they did not make them or had ever seen them before. The trick of the merchant is to keep the people blind in this way, so that they can take the difference between the price at which they buy and that for which they sell.

You can see, my dear friend, why, for them, there is no place for the Jew. Our money, even when lent out for interest, merely remains as money and comes back to us as money. Unlike these Christian merchants, money does not suddenly turn into something else that pretends it is not money. Antonio calls our money, our Jewish money, 'barren'. How can it be barren if it breeds in the way of more money?

For all his talk of refusing to be 'neither a lender nor borrower', he came to me for a loan. A loan, not for business you understand, but for love! How fragile is *his* new practice! He talks of money 'breeding', but how successful is the intercourse when his money, or as he calls it, 'his goods' sit nowhere other than in the bright blue sea, at the mercy of the heavens and of the pirates? No, he still needs us Jews and our money. Or so I thought . . .

Yes, he needs our money, but all of it . . . and now. His new way of making wealth depends on all the people buying and selling. Because all people do not do this, he is limited. He also runs the risk that all his money could disappear in one rough night on one rough ocean. If only I would have understood his merchant's situation. I would have acted so differently.

In the end Antonio robbed me. He and his like robbed me of all my money. If they had come like thieves in the night and taken it, at least that would have been open and, dare I say, honest. But such an action they would see as unchristian. Instead, they stole it with deceit; they stole it in the name of love – they stole it in the name of their Lord; and I was a party to it.

When I saw Antonio come into my house ready to make an agreement, my heart leapt. 'Now I have him', I thought, and I did. But, oh, how I missed my chance; how stupid I was. If only I had acted as a Jew! Instead I acted as a Christian; can I now complain that I was judged like a Christian?

As you know, I lend money free of favour. What do I care about the person who stands in front of me; what do I care if he is Jew, Christian or Moor, whether he be left-handed or right-handed? All I care is that the person is good; and by 'good' all I mean is that he is good for the debt. I sit as with an equal and discuss the agreement, and sign, seal and deliver it within the bond. If the debt cannot or will not be met when it is due, then I go to court, appeal to the law and expect, nay, demand, that the law treat me as I have treated it, with respect and with justice. That, as you more than others know, my dear friend, is the Jew's greatest and most magnificent achievement – the creation of the law, and the subservience of all in the face of it. Where, I ask you, would the world be, without this greatest of miracles?

If I had acted under the law in my dealings with Antonio, what a different story could now be told. Knowing that his ventures were at the mercy of the gravest of risks, and knowing the desperation of his love for Bassanio, I could have charged whatever interest I wanted with such a forfeit that, had his ships been a day late, he would have been ruined, and it would have been my satisfaction to see that day.

But, oh, what a fool I was. In front of me I saw, not a man like all others, not a man of more or of less means, but Antonio – a Christian and a merchant who had made enemies of me and my people. My passion obstructed my vision and my thought.

I could not see that in baiting him, it was he who set the trap and that I walked into it, as I said, blindly but with my eyes wide open. These Christians, what do they know of setting prices and charging interest justly, according to the law, free of personal involvement? No, they sneer at interest (as if it were different from profit!) and, so he tells me, they give money in the spirit of friendship and love. Indeed, in their new merchants' corporations they set their prices in agreement one with the other and measure it not by justice in the face of the law, but by love in the face of their Lord. Oh, how this elite and the rabble act in the same way.

That was the next step in my own undoing. I, Shylock the Jew, blasphemed against our own law, and acted as a Christian. In place of the justice inherent in our law, I was willing to use the cover of the law to wreak vengeance, but under the thin veneer of kindness, friendship and love. It was only later that I realised just how strong was the relation of Christian love to Christian vengeance.

I told Antonio that I would deal in kindness with him, contrary to my legal and just habits. And, in this so unjewish way of dealing, I thought I would be better at being a Christian than Antonio! What a mistake I made.

I told him that in the spirit of friendship I would forsake all interest and, should the debt not be met, merely ask for a pound of his flesh. Of course, I knew that this would mean his death; what I did not realise was that I was staking my own life as well.

The day of the forfeit finally arrived. In the meantime, my daughter Jessica eloped with a Christian and took on his religion. This event compounded my desire for vengeance to that which I felt toward that Christian-merchant Antonio.

I went into court that day with vengeance in my heart, but, of course, to me and to the court I pleaded that vengeance in the name of justice. After all, I argued, the date for repayment had arrived, the money could not be returned to me, so, as the law demands, I must be allowed to take my pound of flesh from him as was written in the bond to which Antonio agreed and signed as a freeman.

The judges, those trained in the law, and only the law, despite some whining for clemency, had no alternative but to agree that I was in the right. All victory was to be mine. It was then that Portia arrived on the scene; asked by the court to arbitrate. Why could not they themselves decide? Surely, the law is the law?

Oh, how Christian love appears! Did she come into court dressed as that which she was – love and virtue? No, she came in (as did I) as a charade; she came disguised as a lawyer. What chance did law and justice, those noblest of Jewish values, stand in the face of her Christian values of love and revenge?

Oh, what pretence of justice she made! I should have seen what was about to be visited on me. In the guise of Justice she asked, not Justice's question, who was defendant and who was plaintiff? Instead, she asked who was merchant and who was Jew? As if she did not know the answer! She continued her masquerade as the blindness of law when she pretended not to see the difference between me in my gabardine and the merchant in his finery.

Still masked, in this court of law, she then, with eloquent words, pleaded with me in the name of mercy and charity. Oh, those vile Christian virtues through which their love of man is met. What have I, a man of the law, to do with love or mercy? What does a Jew know of love? I do not *love* my fellow man, I have too much respect for humanity to love a man. I treat a man with respect, as my equal, no matter who he is. Because of my lack of love, a lack I am proud of, can I, a Jew, show mercy? Nay, to show that noble, Christian virtue, you need to be above another, to patronise him with your pity. If I am above a Christian, it is in the name of justice. I demand justice, I expect to be judged according to it, not according to love.

But, if the truth be known, what justice could I demand? Had I not given up my right to justice when I bargained with Antonio in the name of friendship, but with a heart of vengeance? Had I not made a mockery of law when I attempted to force into it what does not belong there? Can I complain that I was treated in the same way?

How quickly Christian mercy turns to vengeance, yet all in the name of love! At my refusal to show 'love for my fellow man', how speedily love turned to hate. How fast I was to suffer the violence of love spurned.

Using legal arguments full of spite and malice, Portia, that gentle lady, spat out her decision. I may take my flesh, but not a drop of his blood must be spilled. The flesh was mine, the blood was his – as if the two could be separated. One of us had to yield, and, in the face of this court of love and vengeance, it was to be me. And so the precedent was set.

Not content with permitting her to make judgment, they then left it to Portia to speak of punishment. And what punishment. Not the punishment of law and of justice, such notions had flown out of the room, chased by the spirit of love! It was the punishment of love: all I had was to be its own. One half was to the state, to Venice, the other half to Antonio. I had been robbed in Portia's court of all I possessed.

Once dispossessed in this manner, what use did they have for a Jew? To show the measure of my new worth, they told me who I really was and who they really were. I was told that I was an alien who had threatened the life of a citizen, and must pay accordingly. An alien! All my life I had lived in Venice, entering into contracts, paying taxes, yet, I was called an alien. But was I an alien of the state, or was I an alien of a community of love? Or had one become the other? Love and vengeance had overcome law and justice and, dressed in its mantle, continued to act, but with such a different heart.

In this name of love, so unlike that of justice which stands between the wrongdoer and the wronged to temper the feelings of vengeance, in love's own name, the one wronged, Antonio, was to extend further humiliation. In his blend of Christian love and merchant avarice he made me the trustee of my own money. For whom was I to hold this money so it earnt all the more, but without its true owner becoming visible? I was to hold it for my Christian daughter and her Christian husband until my death. If for no other reason, how I desire to live forever!

Finally, Antonio confronted me as the victor faces the vanquished. I lay before him and waited. He could take my life if he so desired. After all, what is a Jew to him after his money and his law have been stolen. And took my life he did; but in a, oh, so gentle, Christian way! Speaking out of mercy, he killed me by bading me to become Christian. By this simple act of death and resurrection, was I no longer to be a Jewish alien in a Christian world?

I could stand no more and left that room of deceit, trickery and hypocrisy.

How, I wonder, my dear friend, will this tale be told to those not present?

Will Portia and Bassanio, lying in their bed of sublime love, readily admit the tricks they played? Will they acknowledge the role of the Jew, of whom they so kindly disposed, in allowing them their peace and happiness? And will Bassanio ever tell the fair Portia that he sought to woo her, not only for her love, but so as to use her wealth to repay Antonio for his first 'gift'?

When Antonio is thanked by Lorenzo and Jessica for the money he has procured for them, will he tell them, *will he tell himself*, of the cost to himself that lay behind that gift of love? Or will he see the Jew in himself even as he congratulates himself for killing Shylock, the old Jew?

And will all of the nations of Christianity ever realise that for them to live in ideal love and communion among themselves, as one perfect community, so as to create their Christian heaven on earth and call it the 'world of justice' – that for such a prize somebody else will need to be seen to pay for their earthly sins, including, of course, the sins of human necessity? And pay we do! Will it now always be us, my dear friend? Will it from this day be the Jews who pay this cost of Christian love, and who will be the water in which they cleanse their vengeance when they find, time and time again, that they themselves must wash their dirty Jewish hands so as to keep their Christian hearts clean.

As for me, I left the court and found that I had done as they willed. I had already become a Christian. But tell me, am I, now with a simple act of baptism, with the rule of a Christian court, more of a Christian or less of a Jew than I was before? As I walk with a cross around my neck, speaking to my noble fellow Christians in words of love and mercy, I shall never forget what else has been taught me – that vengeance is love by another name. Yes, my friend, I was killed as a Jew, but no more than Antonio a Christian. Who now can separate the flesh from the blood?

Introduction

Critical theory has always been interested in antisemitism. It has seen antisemitism as one of the central problems of the modern age. It is frustrating, therefore, that it has not always theorised the problem satisfactorily. It has correctly identified the historical connection between emancipation and antisemitism, but it has remained in thrall to the explanatory tenets of the antisemitic worldview, including the naturalising of social categories and the denial of subjectivity that comes with this naturalising. Until critical theory emancipates itself fully from the object of its critique, its ambitions remain unfulfilled. This book is my contribution to this emancipation project.

I originally began this project towards the end of the last century. At the time I was interested in a sociology of antisemitism, and I investigated the way critical thinkers from Marx to Bauman theorised antisemitism's origins, rises and falls.[1] Needless to say, I found some thinkers more insightful than others, some ideas more compelling than others, and some I thought were downright dangerous. From time to time, over the last 10 or so years, I presented at conferences or workshops various aspects of my thoughts about this work, but until about a year or so ago, with a combination of factors ranging from the fall of the Berlin Wall and the loud but premature claims of the end of modernity, it seemed as if, for all intents and purposes, antisemitism and the Holocaust were falling into their rightful place as history. My work was interesting from a theoretical or historical perspective only. There were some fears of a resurgence of antisemitism in the 'new' countries of Central and Eastern Europe, but these fears were assuaged by explanations that cast this antisemitism as a remnant of the past, as a display of the old, discredited, nationalist antisemitism that, with these countries' integration into Europe, would dissolve into the broader democratic currents that membership in Europe would bring. (On the whole, I think, with some reservations, that this is indeed the case.) Indeed, it may not be too far fetched to say that, at that time, not only was antisemitism a thing of the past, but, at least in 'the West',

---

1 *Critical Theories of Anti-Semitism*, 2000, PhD Warwick University.

the Jews were 'flavour of the month'. At a time when we were all victims, the Jews were the victim *par excellence*, both innocent and ethical.

Despite the comfort that ought to have come with the disappearance of antisemitism, I remember at the time feeling distinct discomfort with this post-Holocaust version of *jude-bonus*. Being a critical reader of Nietzsche, I couldn't quite escape a pervading sense of unease. The word *ressentiment* kept coming to mind. I could not quite shake the idea that, what is loved one minute, can be hated the next. It was this idea of *ressentiment* that I saw in Arendt's comments about how once one has loved vice, one seeks to expunge it completely and totally. (One need only think of Weimar in general and Berlin in particular.) I remember giving a paper on this theme some years back at the Critical Legal Studies Conference in the UK. Through a critique of Lyotard, I argued that the more 'the Jews' are presented as 'the ethical', the more danger there is that those who believe such a preposterous idea will be disappointed when the truth comes out. Jews are in and of the world, I argued, and so are as 'ethical' or not ethical as anyone else. There is something both distasteful and malignant about the idea that Jews are the 'light unto the nation'. Not only, moreover, would people be disappointed with 'the Jews', but they would become doubly disappointed because of their (mainly self-induced)[2] feeling of being duped. As I said, this paper was written some time ago and, it seems to me that in 2007 my fears of *ressentiment* have come to pass. Antisemitism is no longer of historical or theoretical interest only. The work of critical thinkers about antisemitism is no longer about history. Part, but only part, of this current work is to trace the development of this state of affairs. To do so I go back to the very beginning.

What struck me most, as I worked 15 years ago on critical theories of antisemitism, was a double neglect. The first was the relative overlooking by legal scholars of what critical theory had to say about antisemitism and/or the Jewish question. I was struck by the extent to which critical thinkers had engaged with these issues from the dawn of modernity onward,[3] yet whilst a great deal of work had been done on the work of these thinkers as a whole, I could find relatively little that made specific reference to antisemitism (and the Holocaust).

The second neglect was neglect of contemporary comment upon the extent to which these critical accounts of antisemitism framed their discussion through a critique of modern law and modern rights. Almost all of the thinkers discuss in some way the collusion of law with antisemitism. I was surprised, in other words, not only by the amount of light that a critical

---

2 I say 'mainly self-induced' since it is the case also that it was a perception that, as a self-representation, was left unchallenged.
3 These contributions roughly mirror the timescale of Arendt's discussion of the 'long' nineteenth century up to 1914 – with its three decades of 'golden years' as well as the 'silence' from 1948 to 1961 and from 1961 (though less so) to the 1980s.

appraisal of law could throw upon understandings of antisemitism, but also by the extent to which a critical account of antisemitism could illuminate understandings of law. Rather surprisingly, this situation remains similar today.

Perhaps the most obvious way for me to explain what I mean by 'critical' thinking is to use antisemitism as my illustration. In contradistinction to the idea of 'eternal antisemitism' or to the liberal idea that modern antisemitism was a remnant of pre-modern religious superstition, critical accounts of antisemitism place it directly in the context of modern political emancipation. In refusing to treat antisemitism as the 'longest hatred' (whilst, at the same time, not denying that history), all the thinkers discussed here identify, or believe they have identified, *something* about the modern era in general and emancipation in particular that brings with it a specific Jewish dimension. However, in tracing the trajectory of this thinking, it becomes increasingly clear that, in a manner reminiscent of Adorno's and Horkheimer's *Dialectic of Enlightenment*, what begins as *critical* comes to take on the characteristics of the object of critique itself.

The paradox of this development, or inversion, within critical thought is illustrated when we locate antisemitism within the praxis of emancipation and its expression through law and legal rights. Jewish emancipation was meant to spell the end of anti-Jewish hostility and so it is the limits and failings of *emancipation* that are deemed responsible for the appearance of antisemitism. However, the more those limits and failings are weaved into the fabric of emancipation, the more antisemitism appears inevitable. In this way, despite critical theory's stated aim of reinforcing the *social* origins of apparently natural categories, it ends up by reproducing the very naturalness it seeks to challenge. Implicit in this re-naturalising of antisemitism, modern antisemitism takes on the hue of a 'law of nature'. This perspective reveals interesting links between antisemitism's political expression in its relation to emancipation, its legal expression through rights and jurisprudence, and its social expression as representations of subjectivity. Despite what some of the critical theorists here seem to suggest, antisemitism could not exist without antisemites or Jews and the subjectivity of these actors in realms of the political, the social and the legal are important in understanding its expression.

This work is thus organised around these three elements of critical accounts of the relationship between law, antisemitism and the Holocaust. The first element is emancipation, and I attempt to uncover the way in which critical theory unhelpfully moves from conceiving of emancipation as complicit in the creation or perpetuation of antisemitism as its natural outcome. The second element is the place of the ethical within critical thinking about antisemitism. The third problematic is the question of subjectivity. I explore the creation, dissolution and expression of antisemite and Jew through both legal and non-legal manifestations.

The first two essays reflect on the relationship of Enlightenment and emancipation praxis to law, antisemitism and the Holocaust. The first offers an extended discussion of Karl Marx's *On the Jewish Question* (Chapter 1) and the second an investigation of the reflections of Adorno and Horkheimer, Bauman and Agamben on law, antisemitism and the Holocaust (Chapter 2). I argue that Marx's aim to highlight the social basis of seemingly natural phenomena – including rights, money, Jews and Christians – is reversed in the later accounts. The distance between them can be marked by the shift from the equivocal belief that 'everything solid melts into air' to the unequivocal pessimism of a modern era whose ideals have petrified into the impenetrable quality of stone.

In this way, I show how naturalising antisemitism means naturalising 'the Jews'. It is here where, far from 'everything melting into air', the entire edifice of the modern era appears, not only certain and fixed, but petrified, dead and decaying.

It was in the face of this petrifaction that critical thinking turned to 'the ethical' as a way out of the impasse it had created for itself. Against the fixed and implicated categories of law, logos and rationality, critical theory offered ethics and aesthetics as a means both of explaining antisemitism and the Holocaust and of neutralising its resurgence. In Chapter 3 ('The absence of contradiction and the contradiction of absence: law, ethics and the Holocaust'), I argue that the turn in critical thinking is not so different from what went before it. 'The ethical' I argue, is more than a passing resemblance to the positivism and naturalism it believes it has rejected. More worryingly, this jurisprudence of 'the ethical' recognises neither this fact nor its implications.

Staying within the domain of the ethical, Chapter 4 ('Antisemitism and emancipation: the *ressentiment* of loss') illuminates the equivocal role that *ressentiment* plays in critical accounts of law, antisemitism and the Holocaust. Drawing on the work of Nietzsche, Sartre, Lyotard and Agamben, I trace the ways in which the abject rejection of emancipation brings with it not only a *ressentiment* against 'modernity' or 'emancipation', but also against those who claim, like Jews, a 'specific' experience of a universalised history.

The idea of 'petrifaction' is at the centre of the third and final section on subjectivity. Naturalised antisemitism, both predating and a product of modern emancipation, means that it and its subjects, the Jews, appear with the force of nature. My critique of the naturalisation thesis must therefore include an examination of its subjects, both as concepts and as actors. Critical theory postulates the gradual, but notable, disappearance of the figure of the *antisemite*. The two essays in this final section question this view. Chapter 5 ('The slave, the noble and the Jew: reflections on Section 7 of *On the Genealogy of Morals*') proposes that the claim to a denial of subjectivity, the 'desire not to be', rests ultimately, if paradoxically, upon an almost excessive expression of subjectivity. Chapter 6 ('The jurisprudence of Nazi monumental architecture') explores this paradox further by bringing to light the nature of the subjectivity that is expressed in Nazism's adoption of the 'neoclassical' style.

The final essay is a review of Hannah Arendt's study, 'antisemitism'. As I do with the work of other critical theorists, I offer a critique of her approach to understanding antisemitism, but I offer it by way of a conclusion to this book because Arendt's account of antisemitism avoids many of the pitfalls I identify in the other works. Arendt emphasises the equivocality of emancipation and rights. She remains alert to the social and political underpinnings of antisemitism and she refuses to treat the Jews as passive bystanders to history. At a time when an increasing number of thinkers are rediscovering Arendt's political philosophy, I wish to encourage rediscovery also of her iconoclastic understanding of modern antisemitism.

I mentioned at the beginning of these comments my sense of an upsurge of *ressentiment* in matters related to antisemitism and the Holocaust. I hope that this study offers some reflection on how and why this may be the case.

Chapter 1
Karl Marx: dissolving the Jewish question

I begin this study with *On the Jewish Question* by Karl Marx (1818–1883). Aside from it being one of the earliest contributions, the themes addressed by Marx continue to form the contours of the debate. Most important amongst these strands are, first, Marx's insistence that critical thinking bring to light the historical and social underpinnings of what appear as natural phenomena. Second, is the equivocal attitude he adopts to rights as an expression of modern emancipation and the open possibilities of the future. Third, is the presentation of antisemitism as an expression of *ressentiment* against the Jews as the *representatives* of the modern era.

Karl Marx's contribution to a critical theory of antisemitism consists of the two essays that together comprise his article *On the Jewish Question*. I will argue that in defending the cause of Jewish emancipation, Marx seeks to dissolve the Jewish question into one aspect of a critique of the nature of political emancipation in general. Marx criticises the leading Berlin left Hegelian, Bruno Bauer, for seeking to exclude Jews from entry into the modern nation state. He illustrates that the reasons upon which Bauer relies to exclude the Jews apply equally to those whom Bauer deems deserve entry. I also argue that despite his critique of political emancipation Marx does not abandon it. Finally, I will argue that the nature of Marx's defence of Jewish emancipation points to the potentiality for a modern and virulent form of anti-Jewish hostility – antisemitism.

Even though Marx had intended to contribute to the debate on the Jewish question for at least a year prior to the publication of *On the Jewish Question*, his immediate motivation was provided by the publication of two anti-emancipationist and antisemitic tracts by Bruno Bauer.[1] Consequently, Marx's article can be read as an attack on Bauer's leftist antisemitism and Bauer's work provides the reason why Marx's *On the Jewish Question* presents itself as a critique of the idealism of the Young Hegelians.

In *The Jewish Question*, Bauer argued against the Jews being granted

---

1 Bauer, 1843a and 1843b.

either political rights (the Rights of the Citizen) or civil rights (the Rights of Man) on three grounds. First, he said the granting of rights depends upon the Jews renouncing their religious beliefs and adopting atheism. Second, he said that, were the Jews to be emancipated *as Jews*, their 'particularism' (their 'restricted nature') would always dominate over the universalism that he saw as the essence of political and civil rights. Third, he claimed that the Jews had remained outside the historical development that led from Christianity to 'Christianity in dissolution' to human emancipation. In this way, Bauer produced a critique of the Jewish question that rests ultimately on a critical theology and the idealism that such a method implies.

In criticising the first of Bauer's arguments, Marx challenges that which Bauer identifies as a specifically Jewish situation. Bauer wrote:

> [T]he *Jew* will recede behind the *citizen* and be a *citizen*, in spite of the fact that he is a Jew and is to remain as Jew; i.e. he is and remains a *Jew* in spite of the fact that he is a *citizen* and lives in universal human conditions, his Jewish and restricted nature always triumphs in the long run over his human and political obligations. The *prejudice* remains, even though it is overtaken by *universal* principles. But if it remains, it is more likely to overtake everything else . . . The Jew could only remain a Jew in political life in a sophistical sense, in appearance; if he wanted to remain a Jew, the mere appearance would therefore be the essential and would triumph, i.e. his *life in the state* would be nothing more than an appearance, or a momentary exception to the essential nature of things and to the rule.
>
> (quoted in Marx, 1992, p 214; emphasis in the original)

Marx agues that this 'mere appearance' is in fact a *universal* condition and arises, not for any *theological* reason, but is a consequence of the (*secular*) nature of political emancipation itself. Consequently, Bauer's anti-Jewish stance applies as much to those to whom he grants the right to have rights as it does to the Jews themselves. In this way Marx begins his task of dissolving the Jewish question by denying a specific 'nature' of the Jews.

> We humanise the contradiction between the state and a *particular religion*, for example Judaism, by resolving it into the state and *particular secular* elements, and we humanise the contradiction between the state and *religion in general* by resolving it into the contradictions between the state and its own general *presuppositions*.
>
> (Marx, 1992, pp 218–19; emphasis in the original)

In achieving the dissolution of the Jewish question, Marx reformulates the question of the relationship of the Jews to political emancipation:

> Bauer asks the Jews: Do you from your standpoint have the right to demand political emancipation? We pose the question the other way round: Does the standpoint of political emancipation have the right to demand from the Jews the abolition of Judaism *and from man the abolition of religion*.
>
> (Marx, 1992, p 216; emphasis added)

To his own question, Marx answers in the negative.

Drawing on the example of certain North American states, Marx illustrates that the political emancipation of religion does not entail the emancipation of *man* from religion, but rather the *emancipation* of the *state* from religion. This apparent contradiction, Marx explains, arises because *political* emancipation is not synonymous with *human* (that is, social) emancipation (through which humanity would have thrown off the conditions that makes religion a possibility in the first place). Thus, political emancipation represents an individual's freedom from religion only in an indirect, mediated and abstract manner:

> The attitude of the state, especially the *free state* to religion is still only the attitude to religion of the *men* who make up the state. It therefore follows that man liberates himself from a restriction through the *medium of the state*, in a *political* way, by transcending this restriction in an *abstract* and *restricted* manner, in a partial manner, in contradiction with himself.
>
> (Marx, 1992, p 216)

Marx explains the nature of this contradiction with reference to the institution of private property. On the one hand, private property is abolished *politically* when it ceases to be relevant as a qualification for the right to vote. However, this does not mean that private property itself is abolished; it continues to exist and exert its influence but remains in the realm of civil society where it is perceived as a private (that is, apolitical) matter. Marx implies the same is the case for religious belief, be it Judaism or Christianity.

In this way, the contradiction that Marx notes in Bauer's work, 'the state can have emancipated itself from religion even if the overwhelming majority is still religious' (Marx, 1992, p 218) has been explained by the secular nature of political emancipation. Consequently, Marx has countered Bauer's antisemitic idea that the Jews cannot be emancipated *as Jews* and that they must first renounce their own religious affiliation. He illustrates, first, that one's religious belief *in general* is no bar to membership in the state, to a person being granted the Rights of the Citizen, and, second, that of itself, religion does not represent a unique problem, but is expressive of a *general* contradiction between the state and civil society.

Bauer's further claim, that the Jew's alleged 'particularism' will always dominate over 'his human [i.e. universal] and political obligations' so that his *'life in the state* would be nothing more than an appearance, or a momentary exception to the essential nature of things and to the rule' (quoted in Marx, 1992, p 214; emphasis in the original) is also dissolved by Marx through his discussion of a further general condition of political emancipation. Here he points to the nature of the *relationship* between the realm of the state (the public realm) and the realm of civil society (the private realm).

Marx observes that the state's characteristic as the realm of universality or human freedom (what Marx terms as 'species-life') only arises through its opposition to the sphere of private and particular interests. Comparing this relationship with that between heaven and earth Marx alludes to the idea that, from the perspective of civil society in which the individual is burdened with a life of toil and struggle, existence in the realm of the state appears as an ideal of freedom that is, as yet, unattainable. However, even though this state of freedom now appears in the secular world,

> [t]he relationship of the political state to civil society is just as spiritual as the relationship of heaven is to earth. The state stands in the same opposition to civil society and overcomes it in the same way as religion overcomes the restrictions of the profane world, i.e. it has to acknowledge it again, reinstate it and allow itself to be dominated by it.
> (Marx, 1992, p 220)

Thus, the member of civil society is also, at one and the same time, a member of the state. In this way, Marx argues, this divided individual, 'leads a double life . . . not only in his mind, in his consciousness, but in *reality*' (Marx, 1992, p 220).

> He lives in the *political community*, where he regards himself as a *communal being*, and in civil society, where he is active as a *private individual*, regards other men as means, debases himself to a means and becomes a plaything of alien powers.
> (Marx, 1992, p 220)

However, since political emancipation leaves civil society 'uncriticised', the bourgeois[2] perceive their *material* life (that is, their life in civil society as private individuals) as their *real* and *natural* existence. In this way, their life in the state, their life as citizens will always appear to them as an ideal, as something that could only occur once they have left the conditions of their individuality behind. In other words, the bourgeois see their own citizenship in *ideal* and *abstract* terms. Thus, on the one hand, where the individual:

---

2 In this context Marx uses this term to mean the individual as a member of civil society.

> regards himself and is regarded by others as a real individual he is an illusory phenomenon. In the state, on the other hand, where he is considered to be a species-being, he is the imaginary member of a fictitious sovereignty, he is divested of his real individual life and filled with an unreal universality.
>
> (Marx, 1992, p 220)

Through this analysis of the relationship of the state to civil society, Marx has illustrated that the situation that Bauer attributes solely to the Jews as a consequence of their particularist 'restricted nature' is, in fact, attributable to all members of civil society, *as* members of civil society. Furthermore, he has shown that this contradiction applies not only to religious beliefs, now made a 'private affair', but to the plethora of other phenomena (such as private property) displaced by political emancipation into the realm of civil society. Thus,

> [t]he conflict in which the individual believer in a *particular* religion finds himself with his own citizenship and with other men as members of the community is reduced to the *secular* division between the *political* state and civil society. For man as bourgeois 'life in the state is nothing more than an appearance or a momentary exception to the essential nature of things and to the rule'. Of course the bourgeois, like the Jew, only takes part in the life of the state in a sophistical way, just as the *citoyen* only remains a Jew or a bourgeois in a sophistical way; but this sophistry is not personal. It is the *sophistry of the political state* itself.
>
> (Marx, 1992, p 220; emphasis in original)

Moreover, Marx has achieved his aim of dissolving the Jewish question into the 'general question of the age' by adopting a secular methodology in which the nature of political emancipation itself is called into question, rather than adopting the theological and idealist methodology advanced by Bauer.

It is on the same basis that Marx challenges Bauer's argument against granting the Jews the 'Rights of Man' (that is, civil rights). Bauer's reasons for maintaining the exclusion of Jews from membership within civil society is again grounded in the idea of an alleged Jewish nature. Here he argues that the Jews' 'true nature' will result in their separation from Gentiles and so they would not be able to participate within the human community:

> The question is whether the Jew as such, i.e. the Jew who admits that he is compelled by his true nature to live in eternal separation from others, is capable of acquiring and granting to others the *universal rights of man*? ... As long as he is a Jew the restricted nature that makes him a Jew will inevitably gain ascendancy over the human nature which should join him as a man to other men; the effect will be to separate him from non-Jews.

> He declares through this separation that the particular nature which makes him a Jew is his true and highest nature in the face of which human nature is forced to yield.
>
> (quoted in Marx, 1992, p 227; emphasis in the original)

Drawing on the French and American Declarations of the Rights of Man, Marx observes that far from demanding that one's religion be renounced, the Rights of Man guarantees religious freedoms:

> [t]he incompatibility with the rights of man is so alien to the concepts of the rights of man that the *right to be religious* – to be religious in whatever way one chooses and to practise one's chosen religion – is expressly enumerated among the rights of man. The *privilege of faith* is a *universal right of man*.
>
> (Marx, 1992, p 228)

Having resolved the specific relationship of religious belief to the rights of man in favour of the Jews, Marx challenges Bauer's assumption that the Jews, and only the Jews, on account of the 'restricted nature that *makes* [!] him a Jew', will remain a distinct and separate group. Here, again, Marx's purpose is to illustrate that this allegedly unique situation is, in fact, a universal condition.

To achieve this aim, Marx analyses the same declarations. He notes that the fundamental right which gives meaning to all others, *including the rights of the citizen*, is nothing other than the right to the freedom of private property. Marx defines this right as, 'the right to enjoy and dispose of one's resources as one wills, without regard for other men and independently of society: the right of self interest' (Marx, 1992, p 229).

Marx argues that this basic right reflects the condition of the individual as he is constituted within the realm of civil society. Recognised solely through his ownership of private property, each person is perceived as 'an individual withdrawn into himself, his private interest and his private desires [which, as we have seen, now include one's religious beliefs] and separated from the community' (Marx, 1992, p 230). Indeed, any notion of a communal existence appears from this social perspective as an interference or obstacle to the freedom of the individual in his pursuit of his own particularism. Thus, far from social relations expressing ties of 'species-being', '[t]he only bond which holds [social persons] together is natural necessity, need and private interest, the conservation of their property and their egoistic persons' (Marx, 1992, p 230).

Through this critical examination of the meaning and substance of the rights of man and the attributes of the individual who is their embodiment, Marx has shown that the alleged 'nature' of the Jews, which Bauer saw as the reason for refusing Jews the rights of man, is, in fact, a replication of the 'nature' of rights-bearing individuals themselves. It is a 'nature', moreover, that, far from being inherent in 'man himself' is, in fact, socially and politically constituted.

Finally, by tracing the secular and materialist bases of rights, Marx has also overcome the third element of Bauer's anti-emancipationist argument. Bauer had argued that the Jews should be excluded from the right to have rights because they stood outside the history that 'discovered' them. He states,

> [t]he idea of the rights of man was not discovered in the Christian world until the last century. It is not innate in man. On the contrary, it can only be won in a struggle against the historical traditions in which man has up to now been educated. Therefore, the rights of man are not a gift of nature or a legacy of previous history, but the prize of the struggle against the accident of birth and the privileges which history has handed down from generation to generation. They are the *product of culture*, and only he can possess them who has earned them and deserved them.
> (quoted in Marx, 1992, p 227; emphasis added)

Here, Bauer implicitly refers to the teleological and idealist thinking of Feuerbach[3] through which the history of emancipation was read as a 'progression' from Judaism to Christianity, to what Bauer terms 'Christianity in dissolution',[4] to human freedom. In consequence of this anti-Jewish interpretation, the Jews were seen as an anachronism. Their 'stubbornness' in clinging to an allegedly superseded religion was interpreted as their refusal to join in with the march of human progress. It is this sense that Bauer refers to as the 'discovery' of rights as a 'product of culture'. Consequently, Bauer not only argues that Jews should not be granted rights *as Jews* since their alleged particularity and separateness arises, ultimately, from their 'stubbornness', but also calls on them to renounce their religion.

Marx's answer to the Jewish question is to emancipate the Jews, to grant them the rights of the citizen and the rights of man. With this approach he has shifted the focus of attention away from any allegedly subjective attribute of the Jews onto a critique of political emancipation itself. He has illustrated that the nature of the rights in question and the basis upon which they rest transcend any alleged dichotomy between Judaism and Christianity or between Judaism and a Christianity 'in dissolution' which Bauer believed was the progenitor of rights themselves. Marx has also shown that the Jewish question, by its very nature, transcends any praxis premised upon theological or idealistic considerations and, instead, rests upon an analysis that stresses

---

3 Feuerbach, *Essence of Christianity*, trans. George Eliot, 1957, New York and London; in Carlbach, 1978.
4 Quoted in Marx, 1992, p 235.

the importance of making the idealist consequences of political emancipation a social reality.

Having confronted Bauer's argument that the Jews cannot partake in the earthly appearance of freedom on earth – that is, be granted political and civil rights – Marx challenges Bauer's idea that the Jews are nonetheless responsible for subverting that freedom through their alleged social dominance which occurs through a connection with money and finance. Bauer states, for example:

> The Jew, who is merely tolerated in Vienna, for example, determines the fate of the whole empire through the financial power he possesses. The Jew, who can be without rights in the smallest of the German states, decides the fate of Europe.
>
> (quoted in Marx, 1992, p 237)

And, in a similar vein:

> [It is] a dishonest state of affairs when in theory the Jew is deprived of political rights while in practice he possesses enormous power and exercises a political influence in the larger sphere that is denied him as an individual.
>
> (quoted in Marx, 1992, p 238)

Here, again, Marx dissolves what others claim is an inherent attribute of the Jews into a general condition of civil society brought about in the wake of political emancipation. Marx's response to this line of argument is quite simple. As was discussed above, Marx had argued that in the relationship between the state and civil society, the latter always dominates the former. Consequently,

> [t]he contradiction between the practical political power of the Jew and his political rights is the contradiction between politics and financial power in general. Ideally speaking the former is superior to the latter, but in actual fact it is in thrall to it.
>
> (Marx, 1992, p 238)

Marx argues that the social dominance of money is itself only possible within a social context premised upon the dominance of private property. Here, Marx challenges the idea prevalent in Bauer's thought, and in other 'leftist' thought at the time,[5] that the Jews are responsible for the development of

---

5   An example of this form of anti-capitalist antisemitism can be seen in the work of Proudhon (see, e.g., Marx, 1978). See also the comments in Avineri, 1968, and 'Marx and the economic-Jew stereotype' in Draper, 1977.

money and, in consequence, for the alienation of humanity from nature. His argument on this point is that the social significance of money cannot be detached from the institution of private property – that is, from the same institution from which political and civil rights arise.

As we have seen, Marx argues that, through the medium of civil rights, individuals are abstracted from their concrete existence and are recognised solely as owners of private property. Similarly, money is the medium through which nature is abstracted into 'exchange-value' and so becomes robbed of its specific qualities. Thus, just as rights recognise the individual as an abstract owner of private property and so detach this element from his specific qualities so that exchange between two 'equals' can be facilitated, so does money as the medium of exchange abstract the specificity of nature permitting *its* exchange. This character of money is made possible through its function as a universalising medium of exchange. Marx states (1992, p 239) '[m]oney debases all the gods of mankind and turns them into commodities. Money is the universal and self-constituted *value* of all things'.

Moreover, money, as the medium of value through which the world is commodified and transmuted into private property, represents the manner in which man is alienated from nature. Marx says (1992, p 239) 'money has therefore deprived the entire world – both the world of man and of nature – of its specific value'.

As a medium that exists between the natural world and the social world through making the latter amenable to ownership and exchange as private property, the value of nature is reduced to its value in terms of money. The consequence of this process is that:

> [t]he view of nature which has grown up under the regime of private property and money is an actual contempt for and degradation of nature . . . contempt for theory, for art, for history, for man as an end in himself – is the *actual* and *conscious* standpoint, the virtue, of the man of money. The species-relation itself, the relation between man and woman, etc. becomes a commercial object! Woman is put on the market.
>
> (Marx, 1992, p 239)

In this account of the significance and meaning of money, Marx has illustrated how it is intimately related to private property and so to the significance and meaning of rights. He has countered Bauer's thesis that, whilst rights represent the culmination of a journey which has bypassed and excluded the Jews, money is an allegedly Jewish attribute. He illustrates, in other words, the intimate connection between rights and private property. Thus, for Marx, it is the secular and material emergence of private property that gives rise to both rights and money, each of which in turn is a reflection of the conditions in modern civil society in which individuals are themselves treated in abstraction. In this way, again, Marx has removed from the analysis of money any connection with Jewish attributes, and, instead, focused upon the 'objective' situation of the nature of political emancipation.

As others have noted,[6] Marx frames his analysis of money in the guise of a critique of the 'materialist' basis of Judaism. Whilst this study is concerned with the manner in which antisemitism has been theorised in its relationship to modernity and not with whether particular thinkers were or were not antisemitic, a few comments on this part of Marx's presentation are apposite.

It seems to me that Marx's (perhaps unfortunate) use of Judaism to illustrate his thesis rests upon his desire, not only to challenge Bauer's anti-emancipationist and antisemitic thought, but also to ridicule his methodology. As we have seen, Marx takes issue with Bauer's idealistically-driven explanation of rights as the 'product of (Christian) culture'. He also challenges Bauer's view that since Judaism had been 'superseded', the Jews *as Jews* should not and could not be granted political and civil rights. Overtly referring to an allegedly Judaic tradition of seeing nature as something external to human existence, as something that is of use, but not of value – a view prevalent in much German idealistic thought from Kant through to Feuerbach – and comparing it to bourgeois values, Marx has indicated that Judaism is, and has always been part of history. Indeed, he argues that Judaism and Christianity have, in fact, always existed in relation one to the other. As such, even on Bauer's own terms, it was contradictory to claim the Christian 'parentage' of rights, whilst denying Christianity's role in the development of money.

> The Christian was from the very beginning the theorising Jew. The Jew is therefore the practical Christian and the practical Christian has once again become a Jew ... Christianity overcame real Judaism only in appearance. It was too *refined*, too spiritual, to do away with the crudeness of practical need except by raising it into celestial space ... Christianity is the sublime thought of Judaism and Judaism the vulgar application of Christianity. But this application could not become universal until Christianity as perfected religion had *theoretically* completed the self-estrangement of man from himself and from nature ... Only then could Judaism attain universal domination and turn alienated man and alienated nature into alienable, saleable objects subject to the slavery of egoistic need and to the market.
>
> (Marx, 1992, pp 240–1)

Throughout, Marx highlights, first, the weakness of Bauer's critical and idealist philosophy; second, the fact that modern social phenomena have

---

6 See, e.g., Carlbach, 1978.

overcome or transcended any idealistic dichotomies between 'Judaism' and 'Christianity', and, third – and this point is crucial considering the critical comments directed at Marx – that which Nietzsche would later theorise as the concept of *ressentiment* at the very heart of Bauer's thought.

It would, however, be a mistake to read Marx's critique of political emancipation and rights as completely negative. Although he argues that work still needs to be done in order to achieve full human emancipation, he appreciates the significance of first steps. He states,

> *Political* emancipation is certainly a big step forward. It may not be the last form of general human emancipation, but it is the last form of human emancipation *within* the prevailing scheme of things. Needless to say, we are here speaking of real, practical emancipation.
>
> (Marx, 1992, p 221)

For Marx, the recognition of the individual as a rights-bearing person is a recognition of their equality and freedom that should be welcomed. Yet, because these rights are formal rather than substantive, they leave the space for the future development of antisemitism. In his account of political emancipation, Marx concludes that:

> the perfection of the idealism of the state was at the same time the perfection of the materialism of civil society. The shaking-off of the political yoke was at the same time the shaking-off of the bonds which had held in check the egoistic spirit of civil society from politics. Political emancipation was at the same time the emancipation of civil society from politics, from even the *appearance* of a universal content.
>
> (Marx, 1992, p 233)

He points to the fact that political emancipation has robbed civil society of any universal or communal aspect that, no matter how debased in feudal society, was nonetheless present there. As a consequence of political emancipation in which individuals see their conditions in civil society as their real or true life, any *meaningful* notion of community has disappeared. Instead, socially located individuals are now perceived in their isolation as 'self-sufficient monads' – autonomous and standing alone.

This situation of autonomy is replicated in the nature of modern civil rights whereby the rights-bearing person is abstracted from the various concrete aspects of his or her life in a manner similar to his or her abstraction from the 'materialism of civil society' into the 'idealism of the state'. Consequently, personal factors disappear 'behind' the image of the individual as an owner of private property and the socially recognised person comes to be alienated or abstracted from their full and concrete attributes.

The only means of social relationship available to this individual is that of opposition and struggle in which each person is involved in a war of each against all. Those social relations which take place through the medium of money serve to alienate humanity from the nature of which they are a part. The alienation of 'man' from himself, from others and from nature, are all related 'irrational' aspects of the rule of private property which has emerged as a 'rational' outcome of civil society.

Finally, Marx notes that political emancipation brought with it the dissolution of prior forms of social and political existence in which the individual experienced some form of community. However, with the coming of political emancipation and the separations between state and civil society, universalism and particularism, the alienated individual was thrown into the uncertainties of an unreconstituted civil society. It is at this point that the potential for antisemitism is identified.

In the following chapter, I look at the ways in which future critical thinking on antisemitism failed to escape from the naturalism and rejectionist attitude to emancipation that Marx had challenged and so clearly refuted.

Chapter 2

From critique to positivism: domination and the naturalisation of antisemitism

> Civilization is the triumph of society over nature – a triumph that transforms everything into mere nature.
>
> (Adorno and Horkheimer, *Dialectic of Enlightenment*)
>
> Nothing, in my opinion, could be theoretically more dangerous than the tradition of organic thought in political matters by which power and violence are interpreted in biological terms. As these terms are understood today, life and life's alleged creativity are their common denominator, so that violence is justified on the ground of creativity.
>
> (Arendt, *On Violence*)

Introduction

It is interesting to note the ways in which critical accounts of antisemitism have followed the path set out in Adorno and Horkheimer's critique of the Enlightenment in their study *Dialectic of Enlightenment*.[1] Foremost among the themes of this work was the manner in which the trajectory of Enlightenment praxis begins as a critical force and ends as a conservative one. Adorno and Horkheimer traced this trajectory through the intimate connection they saw between society's actual relations with nature and its conceptual representations of it. In both the material and the conceptual spheres the key for Adorno and Horkheimer was domination; the nature of domination is intimately connected to conceptual domination of nature.

---

1 I cannot recommend highly enough the 2002 translation by Edmund Jephcott (edited by Gunzelin Schmid Noerr). It presents the text clearly and demystifies Adorno and Horkheimer's germinal critique of mystification. For an excellent introduction, see Jarvis, 1998. For a reading of Adorno that illuminates Nietzsche's influence, see Rose, 1978. Frederic Jameson (Jameson, 1990) emphasises Adorno's connection to Marx. Alison Stone offers an excellent review of Adorno and Horkheimer's presentation of nature in 'Adorno and the disenchantment of nature', in *Philosophy and Social Criticism* 32: 2. For accounts of Adorno and antisemitism, see Anson Rabinach, 2002; David M Seymour, 'Adorno and Horkheimer: Enlightenment and antisemitism', 51 *Journal of Jewish Studies* 297.

Understood in this way, nature came to be nothing other than what man said it was.

I identify three distinct phases in Adorno and Horkheimer's articulation of the development from critique to positivism. The first is the period of critique, the Enlightenment's destructions of old beliefs. The second is the ascendancy of natural law through which nature gained the appearance of autonomy, and the third is the dominance of positivism through which nature and politics are reduced to a series of 'brute facts'. At this stage, they become qualities reduced to abstract quantities of measurement, exchange and calculation, and social constructions of nature confront society as nothing other than an external and alien force to which patterns of labour and of life must adapt. It is at this point that the domination of nature inverts into the naturalness of domination.

I will then go on to argue that this threefold staging of Enlightenment praxis can act as a guide to critical accounts of antisemitism over the past 15 to 20 years. In the trilogy of works beginning with *Dialectic of Enlightenment*, moving through to Bauman's *Modernity and the Holocaust* and ending with Agamben's more recent work, we see Adorno and Horkheimer's internal trajectory of Enlightenment praxis and its replication in accounts of antisemitism. I argue that Adorno and Horkheimer's work represents the critical origins of antisemitism, Bauman's the moment of 'natural law', and Agamben's a radical positivism, in which a naturalised antisemitism is dissolved within a general and generalised conception of domination. This positivism is not without its critical moments, however. Even in the most positivistic accounts, we can read the presence of extra-positivist social relations and concepts that testify to the premises of critical thinking.

Adorno and Horkheimer: antisemitism within the dialectic of Enlightenment

Adorno and Horkheimer define the Enlightenment as the moment when, for the first time in history, humanity approached nature consciously, as an object whose operations were to be discovered and manipulated. The motivation, however, for this approach was not entirely innocent. If nature's secrets could be uncovered, then its resources could better be exploited for the benefit of humanity. Society as the realm of necessity could be neutralised. Propitiously, this enlightened scientific attitude to nature chimed well with the economic interests of the ascending bourgeois class. It was an alliance that ensured the fate of one was entwined with the fate of the other.

Although Adorno and Horkheimer concentrate on the negative aspects of these developments they, like Marx, did not overlook their progressive elements. They recognised in the early science of Bacon and others the power to break the preceding centuries' hold on superstition. What concerned them, however, was the re-emergence of superstition within Enlightenment praxis itself. They saw as myth the way in which the rational enlightened understanding of nature is accompanied by its appearance as an external and autonomous power to which humanity had to adapt and resign itself. It is this inversion that is captured in the aphorism, 'Myth is already enlightenment, and enlightenment reverts to mythology' (Adorno and Horkheimer, 2002, p xviii).

This ambivalence within the origins of the Enlightenment appears almost immediately in the evolution of natural science. Natural science accounted for the operations of nature through the discovery of natural laws. The laws of nature meant nature worked with an almost mechanic regularity. Like clockwork, nature ticked rhythmically and repetitively, its operations remaining constant regardless of both time and place. In this age of philosophical and practical experimentation, all that was needed for nature to yield its bounty more efficiently was increased knowledge of these laws.

The paradox of this development was that the more science claimed discovery of nature's laws, the more nature appeared autonomous of the scientist. The laws of nature, it was believed, continued to operate with or without human observation and human presence. The more these laws were discovered, the more humanity become in thrall to their rhythms. As the early Enlightenment discovered objective laws of nature, nature took on an objective appearance. As much as humanity confronted nature, nature confronted humanity.

Enlightenment's relationship with nature was radicalised in the transition from market to monopoly capitalism. Scientifically, this move was accompanied by the intellectual shift from nature to positivism in which nature became only that which can be observed, measured and exchanged. This shift was in harmony with the universalising of exchange brought about by the merging of the realms of production and consumption under the power of large-scale corporations, thereby making the 'autonomy' of the realm of exchange superfluous to requirements.

In this stage any aspect of nature that could not be utilised for the purpose of exchange was discarded as so much metaphysics, now treated as a legacy of superstition. Consequently, from the perspective of this era of monopoly capitalism, the laws of nature, with their emphasis on 'cause and motive', appeared as so much metaphysical humbug when compared with the positivist conceptual schema necessary for universal exchange. Questions of 'why' and 'how' became irrelevant. What is, simply is, as if 'ready made' for its single purpose. Correspondingly, the human nuances that were necessary in the realm of market transactions, such as the human art of persuasion, were treated as the last remnants of an unnecessary and unexchangeable nature, as so much irrational and superstitious hocus pocus. As Adorno and Horkheimer explain,

> On the way toward modern science human beings have discarded meaning. The concept is replaced by the formula, the cause by rules and

> probability. Causality was only the last philosophical concept on which scientific criticism tested its strength, because it alone of the old ideas still stood in the way of such criticism, the latest secular form of the creative principle. To define substance and quality, activity and suffering, being and existence in terms appropriate to the time has been a concern of philosophy since Bacon; but science could manage without such categories.
>
> (Adorno and Horkheimer, 2002, p 3)

And, thus, the adaptation to the rhythms of nature seemingly set in place by the dominance of natural laws which accompanied the era of bourgeois capital was correspondingly radicalised. It is this context that gives meaning to Adorno and Horkheimer's aphorism that to survive man must sacrifice himself. In the need to adapt to these new conditions, men and women, like the Shamans of the past, had no option but to adopt the positivistic characteristics of the nature that now seemed to confront them. Involved in this *fait accompli* was a renunciation of all their specifically natural (that is, human) qualities like individuality, particularity and spontaneity.

Paradoxically, it is at this moment of naturalised domination that the relationship between society and nature is fundamentally breached. Adorno and Horkheimer are insistent that the positivist conception of nature is nothing other than humanity's projection onto it of its own social needs. In place of society's dialectic with nature, therefore, society stands in a 'dialectical' relationship with its own imaginings and its own domination. It is this radical breach with nature and the tautology of this dialectic that has such vast implications for the development of antisemitism.

The most serious casualty of the breach between society and nature is human subjectivity.[2] Subjectivity, Adorno and Horkheimer argue, emerges where the ability to project itself onto nature is met with an ability to reflect on what is returned. It is this activity of projection and reflection that gives rise to a sense of self and other, of an inside and an outside. Adorno and Horkheimer clearly articulate the danger to subjectivity brought about by the rupture of this fragile relationship.

> But even as an autonomously objectified subject it is only what the objective world is for it. The inner depth of the subject consists in nothing other than the delicacy and richness of the outer perceptual world. If this intermeshing is broken, the self petrifies. If it is confined, positivistically, to registering the given without itself giving, it shrinks to a

---

2 It is important to note here that whilst Adorno and Horkheimer see subjectivity as a human attribute, they imply that its existence is socially mediated, in some places, locating its emergence to the era of bourgeois capitalism.

point, and if, idealistically, it projects the world out of the bottomless origin of its own self, it exhausts itself in monotonous repetition. In both cases it gives up the ghost – in this the mind and spirit. Only mediation, in which the insignificant sense datum raises thought to the fullest productivity of which it is capable, and in which, conversely, thought gives itself up without reservation to the overwhelming impression – only mediation can overcome the isolation which ails the whole of nature.
(Adorno and Horkheimer, 2002, pp 156–7)

Caught within this void, this 'subject without subjectivity' (Adorno and Horkheimer, 2002, p 140) is reduced to projecting onto the world nothing but its own domination that, with the demise of the ego, appears as if it emerged from the world itself. Reason and reflection are replaced by paranoia and the world becomes:

a mere occasion for its delusion; it becomes the impotent or omnipotent quintessence of what is projected on to it ... The idea, having no firm hold on reality, insists all the more and becomes the fixation.
(Adorno and Horkheimer, 2002, p 157)

The content of this paranoia is antisemitism; the object of its madness is the Jews and the myth of an all-encompassing Jewish conspiracy. Why it is the Jews that should become the focus for this mass delusion is explained by the shift from bourgeois or market capitalism to monopoly capitalism. In monopoly capitalism, the Jews are cast as representatives of the now defunct realm of the market. The social skills appropriate to the lost realm of exchange are treated now as natural attributes, but they are of a nature that, since it remains unamenable to the new situation, is unstable and unpredictable. This nature appears, in other words, as a threat. Moreover, in an age in which to survive means the renunciation of such attributes, their presence – the Jews – acts as a provocation to those who must deny their nature to survive and as a reminder of the possibility of that former freedom. It is the Jews as provokers and reminders that, for Adorno and Horkheimer, accounts for antisemitism's murderous ferocity. The fascist mass is nothing other than those denied humanity being given the permission, but without the responsibility (for that would be contradictory), to deny that humanity to others.

It is important to note here that although antisemitism is produced from within modern society, its function as a political or social praxis is, of itself, not essential. It serves no direct utilitarian purpose. It is 'a luxury for the masses' (Adorno, 1973, p 2). It allows the repressed, at least from the point of view of monopoly capital, to release their tension by satisfying their desire for domination. From the point of view of power, this discharge of energy onto an innocent agent has the advantage also of leaving the actual structures of domination untouched, if not actually strengthened.

Adorno and Horkheimer's account of antisemitism as an expression of their general thesis of the shift from critical thought to positivism does not, however, entirely break free of this trajectory. It remains beholden to positivism in the way that its critique of conceptual accounts of the world are taken at face value. It is as if these concepts really did envelope completely the reality they sought to present. Nowhere is this point more in evidence than in their treatment of 'the Jews' as a socio-economic concept. And, as such a concept, it masks or denies the presence or existence of the 'non-conceptual' Jews of everyday life.

Correspondingly, in arguing that antisemitism comes into play precisely at the moment of the demise of society and of the subjectivity that accompanies it, Adorno and Horkheimer confuse the naturalist claims for the world made by positivism as if it really did succeed in petrifying all social relations. It is a confusion that runs directly through their account of antisemitism. Antisemitism is given the appearance of a phenomenon that is independent of individual human thought and human action, or, rather, conscious thought and conscious action. As such, it takes on the characteristic of a natural phenomenon, one that in operating behind the backs of humanity remains beyond the grasp of human responsibility and responsiveness.

Although Adorno and Horkheimer do not claim antisemitism to be inherent within Enlightenment itself, its appearance as an integral and 'natural' aspect of the later modern period is enhanced by the epilogue to these events included in the post-war edition of *Dialectic of Enlightenment*.[3] In this additional section, Adorno and Horkheimer argue that even antisemitism has lost its specificity and has been dissolved into the generalised structure of modern domination. Its particularist character has been reduced to a formal and abstract element of a political platform or party ticket; one more 'fact' that can be exchanged for any other. It is in this scheme of things that antisemitism merges indiscriminately into the general conceptual schema.

Zygmunt Bauman: between critical theory and positivism – antisemitism as a law of nature

In this section of the essay I argue that Zygmunt Bauman's influential account of antisemitism can be understood as the midpoint on the trajectory from critical thinking to positivism. I argue that despite Bauman's emphasis on the connection between antisemitism and naturalism and positivism, his work contains the idea of a social realm, similar to the one Adorno and Horkheimer see as the site of critical thinking. We see this realm most clearly

---

3 *Dialectic of Enlightenment* received a limited publication in 1944. It was republished in 1947 with the addition of the last theses (VII) 'Elements of anti-semitism: limits of Enlightenment' (see 'Editor's Notes', Adorno and Horkheimer, 2002, p 217).

in Bauman's characterisation of antisemitism as a phenomenon underpinned by, and expressed through, the language and concepts of natural law.

As we have seen, for Adorno and Horkheimer, the Holocaust[4] is treated as a by-product of the move from bourgeois or market economy to monopoly capitalism. For Bauman, it is presented as the materialisation of a latent *possibility* that is present within the modern quest for order. The Holocaust then becomes the moment in which this tendency within the Enlightenment heritage comes most clearly into view. However, it is important to note that Bauman is explicit in his argument that whilst the Holocaust is made possible by certain facets of the Enlightenment and the modernity that it inaugurated, it was not inevitable. It depended upon a contingent coalescence of situations and circumstances that could or could not be repeated. This distance between modern antisemitism and the Holocaust is itself an expression of the distance between Bauman's account and those that have followed culminating in the dominance of positivism.

Similar to Adorno and Horkheimer, Bauman explains the modern phenomenon of antisemitism through an alliance between power and knowledge. It is important, however, to note the differences between the two approaches. Whereas both share the view that the field of knowledge is to be equated with a naturalist science (even if Bauman does not see it developing into a distinct positivism), they differ in their understanding of the nature of power. As we have seen, for Adorno and Horkheimer, knowledge/naturalist science allied itself with a rising *social* class, that of the bourgeoisie, whereas Bauman connects it with an overtly *political* power, that of the absolutist state. Whilst the consequence of the different alliances is the same – an increasing naturalisation of society and a concurrent naturalisation of the Jews and anti-Semitism – the difference in purpose should not be underestimated. For Adorno and Horkheimer, the purpose of this alliance was for *economic*, that is, social, purposes and its connection with antisemitism somewhat contingent. For Bauman, it was for the political purpose of social *order*, a purpose that, as we shall see, places the Jews, or rather the concept of 'the Jews', centre stage.

These distinctions arise from a difference of opinion concerning the Enlightenment. Bauman appears to accept Adorno and Horkheimer's view

---

4 The concept of 'holocaust' was not used in *Dialectic of Enlightenment*. The executive director of the World Jewish Congress found what he believes may be the first use of the term to describe the Nazis' persecution and genocide of the Jews. Elan Steinberg said that in the foreword of an out-of-print 1944 book, *Legal Claims against Germany*, author Morris Cohen wrote: 'Millions of surviving victims of the Nazi holocaust, Jews and non-Jews, will stand before us in the years to come.' (http://www.jewishvirtuallibrary.org/jsource/Holocaust/term.html). There are, however, mentions of the term dating back to 1941 (US Holocaust Museum). It was in the 1960s that the term gained widespread and popular currency when it was adopted by Elie Wiesel in a review of *The Terezin Requiem* published in the *New York Times*, 27 November 1963. See Najarian, 39 *The Midwest Quarterly* 74 (www.codoh.com/reference/gnawhistory.html).

of the Enlightenment as the moment when humanity first approached nature consciously and instrumentally. His point of departure is in applying that Enlightenment praxis to society, to the idea that human society, and not just 'external' nature, could be made amenable to conscious design.

> [F]rom the Enlightenment on, the modern world was distinguished by its activist, engineering attitude toward nature and toward itself.
> (Bauman, 1991, p 69)

In the sentences that follow, his point of departure becomes apparent.

> Science was not to be conducted for its own sake; it was seen as, first and foremost, an instrument of awesome power allowing its holder to improve on reality, to re-shape it according to human plans and designs, and to assist it in its drive to self-perfection. Gardening and medicine supplied the archmetaphors for human tasks and strategies in the management of human affairs. Human existence and cohabitation became objects of planning and administration; like garden vegetation or a living organism they could not be left to their own devices, lest should they be infested by weeds or overwhelmed by cancerous tissues. Gardening and medicine are functionally distinct forms of the same activity of *separating and setting apart useful elements destined to live and thrive, from harmful and morbid ones, which ought to be exterminated.*
> (Bauman, 1991, p 70; emphasis in the original)

Rather than the naturalisation of society arising indirectly through its relations with the surrounding world of nature, society became for Bauman an object of nature in its own right. Just as for Adorno and Horkheimer knowledge of external nature was mediated through an economic imperative, for Bauman the knowledge of 'social nature' was derived from a political imperative, the dream and possibility of order. At the heart of this project was the ability to distinguish between 'useful' and 'harmful' (Bauman, 1991, p 70) elements, between that which is to be nurtured and that which is to be exterminated; or, to express it more bluntly, to 'split human life into worthy and unworthy' (Bauman, 1991, pp 68–69).

Along with the devising of the initial plan or design for society, science also abrogated to itself its adjudicatory power. It did so on its claims to truth, its claim to see beneath the surface of mere appearances and to reveal the true essence or true nature of things, including humanity. As Bauman makes clear, it was naturalist science and its seeming ability to uncover definitive 'laws of nature' that both created and met this task.

> [W]ith the Enlightenment came the enthronement of the new deity, that of Nature, together with the legitimation of science as its only orthodox

cult, and of scientists as its prophets and priests. Everything, in principle, had been opened to objective enquiry; everything could, in principle, be known – reliably and truly. Truth, goodness and beauty, that which is and that which ought to be, had all become legitimate objects of systematic, precise observation. In turn, they could legitimize themselves only through direct knowledge which would result from such observation ... Human temperament, character, intelligence, aesthetic talents, even political inclinations, was seen as determined by Nature; in what way exactly, one could find out through diligent observation and comparison of the visible, material 'substratum' of even the most elusive or concealed spiritual attributes. Material sources of sensual impressions were so many clues to Nature's secrets; signs to be read, records written down in a code which science must crack.

(Bauman, 1991, pp 68–9)

Modern racist antisemitism then developed and inserted itself into this milieu. What had previously been explained in religious or theological terms came now to be expressed in the naturalist language of 'race' and of 'blood'. Although not unique in their reclassification as a natural rather than a theological concept, Jewishness rather than Judaism, Jews were nonetheless (along with one or two other groups) ascribed the negative status of 'weeds'. Here the connection between antisemitism and natural law becomes overt.

Unlike Judaism, Jewishness ... was located at the level of a natural law (a kind of natural law that ought to be discovered, and then taken account of and exploited for human benefit, but which cannot be wished away, tampered with, or neglected – at least, not without terrible consequences). It is of such a law that Dumont's anecdote was meant to remind his readers: 'Do you want to see how blood speaks?' a French duke once asked his friends. He had married a Rothschild from Frankfurt in spite of his mother's tears. He called his little son, pulled a golden louis from his pocket and showed it to him. The child's eyes lit up. 'You see,' continued the duke, 'the semitic instinct reveals itself straight away.'[5]

(Bauman, 1991, pp 59–60)

Whilst science may provide the means through which Jewish difference was naturalised and racialised, it does not explain why Jewish presence, and ultimately existence, was read in such negative terms. For Bauman, the

5   Whilst Bauman treats this story as emblematic of the cold scientific rationality of racist antisemitism, he overlooks the close human connection through his failure to comment on the relationship between the 'semitic' baby and the antisemitic father. It is this social resentment to one's own acts that, I believe, makes antisemitism such a pernicious force in the modern era (see Arendt, 1979, pp 54–88).

answer to this question lies not only outside the praxis of modern science, but also outside modernity itself. In arguing that modernity 'inherited' the 'concept of the Jew', Bauman distinguishes modern racist antisemitism from its pre-modern progenitors.

The concept of the Jew inherited by modernity was marked by its embodiment of disorder and chaos, or, at least, their potentiality. In religious terms, especially, the Jews' continued existence stood as a question mark to Christianity, just as it did to other modes of communal cohesion. Yet, Bauman argues that this inherent threat posed by the Jews was managed and neutralised by seemingly 'natural' (in the sense of unreflective) rules and rituals governing intercommunal discourse. It was precisely these practices, however, that came to an end with the devastation of the social space that both precipitated and accompanied the birth of the modern nation state. And, as we have seen, what was once regulated with seeming spontaneity now became the object of intervention, of 'planning and administration'. For the first time, Jewish–Gentile problems were recast as a question – or, rather, the Jewish side was posed as a question.

On the one hand, the concept of the Jews as the questioning of all order continued into the modern age. Bauman sees the concept of the Jews as 'flexible and adaptable; an empty vehicle ready to be filled with whatever despicable load 'them' [sic] were charged with carrying' (that is, the non-national nation within the world of nations, 'the stranger' that, in looking in from the outside, questions all certainties and verities, and so on and so forth). On the other hand, the means of re-asserting boundary lines necessary to stop the negative influence of the unhealthy onto the healthy was complicated by the modern slogan of 'equality' and the rights granted in its name. Rights, in other words, recognised no distinction, philosophically or physically, between 'Jewish' and 'non-Jewish' citizens.

> Modernity brought the levelling of differences – at least of their outward appearances, of the very stuff of which symbolic distances between segregated groups are made. With such differences missing, it was not enough to muse philosophically over the wisdom of reality as it is – something Christian doctrine had done before when it wished to make sense out of the factual Jewish separation. Differences had to be created now, or retained against the awesome eroding power of social and legal equality and cross-cultural exchange.
>
> (Bauman, 1991, p 58)

It was in this new, modern situation that natural science proved its worth. Its 'laws of race' claimed and were depended upon to reveal the essence or nature of the Jew that could not but lay hidden under the mask adopted in the name of a false and unnatural 'equality'. And, in so doing, antisemitism took on its modern naturalist, that is, racist, form. As Bauman notes, it is this new scientific aspect that makes the reality of extermination if not an inevitability, then at the very least, a possibility. Quoting Hannah Arendt's 'terse phrase' Bauman notes that,

> Jews had been able to escape from Judaism into conversion; from Jewishness there was no escape.
>
> (Bauman, 1991, p 59)

There is little doubt that the idea of nature being governed by its own inherent rules places Bauman's account within the overarching thesis of *Dialectic of Enlightenment*. For Bauman, nature must have already gained the appearance of something objective, distinct and separate from those who stood in the position of observers. Similarly, whilst the sum of human knowledge was increased by the 'observation' of such laws, their very existence implied a respective measure of resignation or acceptance. Whilst such acceptance did not rule out human manipulation of such laws, it was these laws that came increasingly to be treated as unalterable facts that humanity had no choice but to accept.

On the other hand, the idea that one could observe nature and, with the correct formulations, manipulate it, implied that society still retained at least some space for manoeuvre or autonomous action. True, objective laws limited this manoeuvrability, but they certainly did not hold that humanity was irredeemably in their thrall. It is this mediation between 'humanity' and 'nature' that, when applied to the social context, still offers the basis for the survival of critical thinking. It is within this moment of the dialectic of enlightenment that Bauman's account of modern antisemitism can be located.

So, while Bauman's account is informed by a clear critical perspective, it carries with it the seeds of positivism identified by Adorno and Horkheimer. Most overt is the increasing subsumption of antisemitism within a more generalised notion of domination; the idea that antisemitism must be understood less as a phenomenon on its own terms than as an instance or illustration of broader and more general trends. Understood in this way, antisemitism becomes less a product of *social relations* than the product of a power that is distinct from and imposes itself onto society from without. In this instance, the locus for such power is an extra-social naturalist science that makes the object of its study – society and the humanity that comprise it – in its own image.

This positivism of power in which and through which society and antisemitism are naturalised is expressed equally in the positivist nature of Bauman's conceptual schema. Bauman is quite correct to link the imagery of the garden with modern conceptions of both political and scientific power. This association appears in the gardening enterprises of Hampton Court (along with the geometrical grid of its maze) and of the Palace of Versailles, as well as other numerous instances whereby nature was to be tamed according to human artifice. It is at this time also that the (ordered) garden makes an appearance as artistic and literary settings.[6] A problem arises, however, when this concept is abstracted from its specific historical context. In breaking free from its social and political ties, it acquires the characteristic of a positivist concept – static, abstract, formal and made to represent something alien to itself. A similar fate befalls both the concept of natural science as well as the absolutist state to which it is attached by Bauman.

The problem of abstraction appears in starkest relief in Bauman's use of the concept of 'the Jews'. As we have seen, Bauman's concept of the Jews is a concept posited by naturalist science and imposed on an otherwise invisible group of social actors. This idea that the concept is posited is reinforced by its formal qualities, by its characterisation as an 'empty vehicle'. By treating the 'conceptual Jew' as a construct of power, Bauman divests himself theoretically of any consideration that 'the Jews' could have emerged (either in its naturalist form or otherwise) if not in isolation, then at least in connection with the mundane world of fluid and changing social relations of which Jews, as an empirically present group, were active. Like Bauman's naturalisation thesis in general, his thinking on antisemitism and the Jews appears to exclude what for Adorno and Horkheimer was the very basis of critical thinking, a social reality that was simultaneously expressed through the language of naturalism whilst at the same time offering the basis for its human and historical critique.

However, it is important to recognise that Bauman's account of modern antisemitism, for all its positivist aspects, does not break free entirely of social relations and social concepts. The continued presence of society comes into clearer focus once it is recalled that the very praxis of antisemitism that Bauman identifies came into existence precisely to counter the praxis of political equality and juridical rights brought in the wake of political emancipation. The fact that Bauman reformulates and, in many ways, inverts the relationship between them does not, of itself, mean the disappearance of the social realm.

This continued presence of society is most evident in the rather obvious point that the exercise of power and its articulation as modern racist antisemitism is never detached from a goal or purpose. Bauman keeps the underlying cause that motivates this power constantly in view. Unlike the radical positivism characterised by Adorno and Horkheimer, in which the ideas of 'cause' and 'motive' are dismissed as so much metaphysical humbug, Bauman's thinking articulates a distance or gap that remains between the exercise of power and its objective of the perfect society. Real society can be found in that gap.

It is interesting also to recognise the modern nature of this 'veiled' society.

---

6 See, for instance, 'The Enlightenment's garden', in Till, 1994, pp 33–7.

As Bauman noted, the entire edifice of the Enlightenment praxis of naturalisation emerged to oppose the existing social reality of political equality expressed through abstract juridical right. That from the perspective of modern power such equality and such rights were considered 'mere' appearance should not be equated with their non-existence or even their insignificance. It is this fact, perhaps, that accounts for the imagery of 'application', of a power applied to an *already* existing body, that pervades Bauman's account of modern antisemitism. His emphasis on the bureaucracy, the institution that mediated the relationship between state and society, seems to substantiate this point.

It follows from what has been said that the idea that science had to apply its findings onto something outside of itself points likewise to a social presence. For a Jew to become his or her concept, for example, the one had to be merged with the other. And, of course, the advantage of Bauman's emphasis on the 'conceptual Jew' over that of the 'flesh and blood' or 'day to day' Jew was that he leaves open the possibility of a lack of fit. Those murdered as Jews by the Nazis were as much the product of Nazi definitions as of individual belief or identity. In this way, Bauman's critique of the 'conceptual Jew' and its distinction from social Jews offers a succinct challenge to any belief in a Jewish 'essence'. It also brings to the fore the presence of a social reality that has provided the base for a critical account of not only the 'conceptual Jew' but also of antisemitism as a whole.

It is true, of course, that by presenting modern antisemitism as closely connected to generalised domination brought about in and through the Enlightenment, Bauman makes antisemitism appear as more, rather than less likely to happen. In so doing, he argues that antisemitism takes on characteristics akin to a natural phenomenon. If, as Bauman has argued, antisemitism inheres within the very nature of the 'gardening project' then it becomes a natural aspect of the modern landscape. As antisemitism is uncovered as the essence of modernity, it takes on the appearance of a law of nature. It appears as something inevitable to which, at least as long as modernity continues, society must resign itself.

Considering the nature of his account and his idea that Jewish negativity was present in the mind of the gardeners from the outset, Bauman's naturalisation of antisemitism should not be surprising. However, when he connects the constant presence of modern racist antisemitism and its expression in the Holocaust, Bauman's claims should not be understated. Whilst he argues correctly that the Holocaust could only have occurred in modernity, he insists that modernity is a necessary but not sufficient cause. Just as there is distance between power and society, so too is there the distance between antisemitism and the Holocaust.[7] On this point, it is worth quoting Bauman at length.

---

7 Bauman's emphasis on the presence of the bureaucracy for the machinery of death is telling on this point. Cf Fine and Hirsh, 2002.

It is only too easy to over-react to the apparent bankruptcy of established sociological visions. Once the hope to contain the Holocaust experience in the theoretical framework of malfunction ... has been dashed, one can be tempted to try the 'obvious' exit from the theoretical impasse; to proclaim the Holocaust a 'paradigm' of modern civilization, its 'natural', 'normal' (who knows also *common*) product, its 'historical tendency'. In this version, the Holocaust would be promoted to the status of *truth* of modernity (rather than recognized as a *possibility* that modernity contains) – the truth only superficially concealed by the ideological formula imposed by those who benefit from the 'big lie'. In a perverse fashion, this view ... having allegedly elevated the historical and theoretical significance of the Holocaust, can only belittle its importance, as the horrors of genocide will have become virtually indistinguishable from other sufferings that modern society does undoubtedly generate daily – and in abundance.

(Bauman, 1991, pp 5–6)

And, in treating the Holocaust as a '*possibility*' that modernity contains' rather than a 'paradigm', Bauman remains aware of the equivocations that can be found within his theorising of modern antisemitism.

Giorgio Agamben: power, positivism and antisemitism

It is in Agamben's reflections on antisemitism that the trends toward naturalism and positivism that have been identified in the work of Adorno and Horkheimer and Bauman appear in starkest relief. I argue, however, that despite this transparency, the basis for critical thought – that is, the presence of society and social relations – still remains.

Unlike the other authors discussed here, Agamben has not (at least not yet) addressed the question of antisemitism directly. His reflections on it, however, can be found in a series of works, most notably *Homo Sacer: Sovereign Power and Bare Life, Remnants of Auschwitz: the Witness and the Archive* and *State of Exception*, in which, interestingly, Agamben uses antisemitism as an 'example' or 'paradigm'[8] of a universalist notion of modern domination. The loss of specificity of antisemitism and its dissolution into broader phenomena are symptomatic of an increasingly fatalist attitude toward its presence in the modern world.

My use of fatalism here is intended to bring to mind Adorno and Horkheimer's contention that Enlightenment reverts to mythology. More

---

8 See 'The camp as biopolitical paradigm of the modern', in Agamben, 1995, Part Three; see also Agamben, 2004, Chapter 1.

specifically, it points to the intimate connection between the disenchantment of nature and its re-enchantment; of the association between domination of nature and the seeming naturalness of that domination.

In many ways, Agamben's account of antisemitism draws upon many of Bauman's themes, particularly the theme of the naturalisation of society and the place of antisemitism within it. What does differentiate the two thinkers, however, is less the scientific aspects of this naturalisation than its political dimension. Whereas Bauman places his 'findings' in the context of the state's obsession with and need to act upon achieving an external (that is, social) order, Agamben treats them as absorbed within the nature of modern political power itself. In this way, Agamben presents modern racist antisemitism as a *direct and unmediated* exercise of political and juridical power.

Writing in *Remnants of Auschwitz*, Agamben characterises the social space of the modern nation state as that of a 'biopolitical domain'. 'Biopolitics' is a concept that, in its transparency, captures exactly the fusion between the 'political' and the 'natural' that Agamben sees as the heart of modern domination and modern antisemitism. Biopolitics for Agamben presents an entirely novel mode of governance, one that takes as its subject-matter the biological life of its citizens. Biopolitics, in other words, points to a specifically modern practice in which the very meaning and definition of politics is premised upon an abiding and foundational concern with the natural or 'bare' (that is, biological) life of the subject within its domain.

> The same bare life that in the *ancien regime* was politically neutral and belonged to God as creaturely life and in the classical world was (at least apparently) clearly distinguished as *zoë* from political life (*bios*) now fully enters into the structure of the state and even becomes the earthly foundation of the state's legitimacy and sovereignty.
> (Agamben, 1998, p 127)

At this juncture in the discussion, it is important to emphasise Agamben's difference from Bauman.

As we saw earlier, Bauman's account of what we can now see as a form of biopolitics – an alliance between political power and scientific knowledge – sought to arrest the problem of chaos and disorder brought about by the advent of political emancipation and formal, abstract juridical notions of equality. For Agamben, however, no such tension exists. Rights and biopolitics, political citizenship and *zoë* are elided.

This immediacy between rights and birth, law and nature, accounts also for Agamben's elision of the tension inherent within 'nation state' into the singularity of 'nation'. Recall here that nation is a concept that tended to be understood in more naturalist terms than the 'rationality' of the state.⁹ Agamben explains this collapse of rights into nation, of 'nativity into nationality', as follows:

> Declarations of rights represent the originary figure of the inscription of natural life in the juridico-political order of the nation-state ... The fiction here is that *birth* immediately becomes *nation* such that there can be no interval or separation [*scarto*] between the two terms. Rights are attributed to man (or originate in him) solely to the extent that man is the immediately vanishing ground (who must never come to light as such) of the citizen.
>
> (Agamben, 1998, pp 127–8; emphasis added)

It follows from this depiction, therefore, that the granting of citizenship (now linked to membership of the nation) becomes a decision decided by biopolitics. At stake is no longer a question of *political* membership, but a question of *zoë*, life itself. Here, biopolitics coincides immediately with thanapolitics (Agamben, 1999, p 83).

This immediacy at the heart of biopolitics, the fusion of politics (power) and nature (knowledge), is articulated further in Agamben's choice of the word 'inscription' when he writes of the elision between rights and life. If 'application' (Bauman) requires a pre-existing object, (that is, a human or social being) upon which biopolitics is then *applied*, inscription indicates a more *generative* or *creative* process, in which the nature or 'bare life' is *brought into being* by biopolitics. Biopolitics, in other words, does not limit itself to the inclusion of *birth* as a political matter, but reaches further into the very meaning of life itself. The decision, in other words, of who shall live as a national and who shall not live as a national (in a literal as well as a metaphorical sense) is not to be understood as the application of a set of criteria onto a pre-existing category of people, but is itself produced by that very political decision.

> The link between politics and life ... is not (as is maintained by a common and completely inadequate interpretation of racism) merely an instrumental relationship, as if race were a simple natural given that had merely to be safeguarded. *The novelty of modern biopolitics lies in the fact that the biological given is as such immediately political, and the political is as such immediately the biological given.*
>
> (Agamben, 1998, pp 147–8; emphasis added)

Thus, the elision of political power and knowledge of nature accounts for the arbitrary selections of national citizens. Rather than confronting an external,

---

9 See, e.g., 'The decline of the nation-state and the end of the Rights of Man' in Arendt, 1979 and Sartre, 1995.

'objective' world, biopolitics offers the opportunity to create the world in a manner of its choosing. Indeed, the moment of creation and the moment of evaluation – who shall be a member of the nation (who shall live) and who is to be excluded (who shall not live) – is a decision and an act located solely in the hands of power. The 'subjectivity' of biopolitics means, further, that no decision is final – that, in its omnipotence, biopolitics makes the 'threshold' of inclusion and exclusion eternally indeterminate.

> One of the essential characteristics of modern biopolitics (and will continue to increase in our century) is its constant need to redefine the threshold in life that distinguishes and separates what is inside from what is outside. Once it crosses over the walls of the *oikos* and penetrates more and more deeply into the city, the foundation of sovereignty – non-political life – is immediately transformed into a line that must constantly be redrawn. Once *zoe* is politicized by declarations of rights, the distinctions and thresholds that make it possible to isolate a sacred life[10] must be newly defined.
>
> (Agamben, 1998, p 131)

It is here we see that entire categories of modern political life, including those of 'the Jews', become the naturalised product of an absolutist positing power. The creation, the meaning and the evaluation of 'nature' collapse into one, and critical accounts of antisemitism collapse into the elision of naturalism and positivism.

The nature of biopolitics constrains Agamben's discussion of antisemitism within the context of the 'Nazi state' [*sic*]. From Agamben's perspective, only Nazism made membership of a specific 'race' not only a criterion for membership into the nation, but also one for life and death. If one was not an 'Aryan' one was a 'Jew', and if one was a 'Jew' one was excluded from the nation in every conceivable way.[11] Whilst such a proposition is not without its problems,[12] the question remains, 'Why the Jews'?

From what has been said so far, the answer would appear to turn on sheer capriciousness or the arbitrariness of 'selection' and, in so doing, would at least offer an echo of the sheer arbitrariness of the 'selection' procedures that took place on the ramps of Auschwitz–Birkenau.[13] There is no doubt

---

10 For Agamben, 'scared man' or *homo sacer*, points to his idea of a life that can be killed but not murdered, as one who exists in the 'threshold' of inside and outside (see Agamben, 1998, p 8).
11 On this point, Agamben emphasises the fact that, prior to deportation, Jews were deprived of their national status.
12 E.g., can we talk of Nazism as a 'state' or equate 'race' and 'nation' (see Arendt, 1979). This question reaches beyond the confines of the present essay.
13 For a critical discussion of Agamben's account of Auschwitz, see Mesnard, 2004.

that the attempt by the Nazi regime to identify 'authentic Jews' according to their racial profiling failed miserably so that other, less 'scientific' means were needed, such as membership of synagogues. However, this response would underplay Agamben's central claim for biopolitics: inscribing its naturalised categories onto bare, natural life, rather than through a process of 'application'.

Phrased in this way, it would appear that the only answer to the question is the somewhat tautological response that 'the Jews' were created by Nazism solely for the purpose of their destruction. It is here that the concepts 'the Jews', antisemitism and the Holocaust collapse into one. It is as if the notion of 'cause and effect' that Adorno and Horkheimer see as the last legacy of the era of natural law has finally been jettisoned. All that remains as the premise of explanation is the posited power of the political.

With the specificity of antisemitism dissolving into a more generalised and universal concept of 'domination' comes 'the Jews' and antisemitism (and, implicitly, their destruction, the Holocaust) acquiring the status of an example or a 'paradigm'.

> As the people that refuse to be integrated into the national political body (it is assumed that every assimilation is actually only simulated), the Jews are the *representatives par excellence* and almost the *living symbol* of the people and of bare life that modernity necessarily created within itself, but whose presence can no longer be tolerated.
> (Agamben, 1998, p 179; emphasis added)

To return here to a comment made by Adorno and Horkheimer, it is as if Agamben's treatment of antisemitism and the Jews as a paradigm of the naturalising effect of modern political power has culminated in what they saw as the dream of positivism from 'Parmenides to Russell' (Adorno and Horkheimer, 2002, p 5), the dream of reducing the many to the one. Reduced to a series of abstract formalist concepts born out of a single omnipotent source, the specificity of antisemitism and 'the Jews' (not to mention Nazism) is dissolved within a universalising and universal notion of absolute domination and its concepts fated to everlasting life within an endless chain of exchange.

Treated as if it were a power that truly was external to and autonomous of any historical and social, *human* influence, domination and its sub-sets appear now as nothing other than 'brute facts'; so inherent in the modern era that they appear with the force and fate of nature. Confronted with the final inversion of enlightenment into mythology, the choice that appears to confront us in this re-enchantment of nature appears as simple as it is inevitable. If what is, is nothing other than a totalising and demonic power, then only two options remain, resignation or destruction. Whereas modern domination arose from a destruction out of creativity, Agamben offers us creation out of destruction.

Yet, even here, and almost despite itself, the glimpse of an extra-political, extra-positivist and non-natural basis for antisemitism appears. In the last quote offered above, Agamben raised the question of 'integration', which, in this instance, means the integration within the national political body. Implicit in this formulation is not only the idea of a refusal, or 'Jewish refusal' (albeit one put into their mouths by antisemitism) but also that 'the Jews', even in conceptual form, exist *outside* or *prior* to the exercise of power upon them; that Nazism 'applied' its judgement rather than 'inscribed' it upon a formless 'bare' or 'natural life'. The reference above to the fusion of rights and bare life at the heart of citizenship does not answer this conundrum since, according to its logic, the Jews would have been excluded *prior* to the creation of the juridical nation.[14]

From this observation, it would appear that Agamben attributes to 'the Jews' either an ontological status as existing outside and prior to biopolitics or, like Bauman (and this goes against the grain of his thesis), status as a social concept. The fact that the social and the political may well be absorbed one into the other (the political into the social for Adorno and Horkheimer, the social into political for Bauman), does not deny their separation outside moments of political totalitarianism (that is, Nazism).

Agamben's position as critic, located outside the phenomenon that he is depicting and explaining also evidences this equivocation. This critical positioning also appears in his lecture on the meaning of the 'paradigm'. In proposing that 'it is the phenomenon itself which is original. No more origin, but original phenomenon', and that 'the thing itself being shown beside itself exposed in its own knowability' implies, at the least, that object retains some specificity.

What does seem clear, however, is that despite his insistence on ontology, social categories and concepts remain embedded throughout Agamben's work on the biopolitics of modern domination, even at those moments he identifies with their destruction. We saw this equivocation at play in his discussion of the Jews in the context of Nazi Germany. In other words, there is a particularity and specificity, a *social actuality*, that remains to continue its critical work even within a theory that denies its existence.

Conclusion

Underlying each of these three accounts is the idea that the stronger humanity's domination of nature is, the more domination appears natural. It is of the utmost importance to note that this dialectic does not refer to

---

14 For an interesting discussion of the question and place of rights in *Homo Sacer*, see Andreas Kalyvas, 'The sovereign weaver: beyond the camp', in Norris, 2005. Andrew Norris' 'Introduction: Giorgio Agamben and the politics of the living dead', is particularly useful.

nature's domination of humanity. On the contrary, each of these accounts emphasises that humanity's attempt to dominate nature results in its further alienation from nature. In short, humanity is in a relationship with itself or, at least, with humanity's projection of itself. The move from critical theory to positivism has thus been matched by the erosion of the distance between that which projected that conception and the nature from which it alienates itself. The further the move along this trajectory, the more humanity faces nothing other than its own imaginings.

Two final points emerge that need clarifying. The first is that critiques of antisemitism take on the characteristics of antisemitism. Antisemitism appears as something inherent within Enlightened modernity. Corresponding to this assimilation and elevated to the status of 'paradigm', the specifics of antisemitism are replaced by a formal and abstract concept that is increasingly applied to myriad equally distinct and unique situations. What is lost, in this retreat of critical theory into positivism, is not only an understanding of actual worldly events, but the particularities of antisemitism, and the particularities of the social worlds that bring it into being. Most importantly, lost also is the means through which it can be acknowledged and confronted.

The second point is that regardless of the extent to which domination is presented as natural, the mere fact that it is recognised and evaluated as such means that, despite all claims to the contrary, the space for both critical thinking and critical action remains. It is this social and historical space that provides the basis for one of the limited goals of critical theory, to bring to the fore the social reality mystified and mythologised through the prism and the concepts of 'the natural'.

Chapter 3

The absence of contradiction and the contradiction of absence: law, ethics and the Holocaust

Introduction

It may not be too much of an exaggeration to note that the history of critical theory can be characterised by one overarching debate.[1] On the one side, and originating with Kant, is the grounding of critique of modernity upon *absence*. On the other side, and beginning with Hegel, the premise of critique is contradiction. Kant's work is structured around the absence of full cognisance of the moral law, whilst, for Hegel, ethical life is presented as the reconciliation of contradictory elements already present in the world. In recent years, the terms of the debate have shifted markedly in favour of absence.

An important catalyst for this contemporary imbalance is traceable to the occurrence of what has come to be known as the 'Holocaust'.[2] Confronted with the sheer horror and magnitude of the crimes committed, many critical theorists committed to contradiction lost their confidence and moved, often with regret, to the side of 'absence'. Most emblematic of this despair is Adorno's *Negative Dialectics* and, in particular, his discussion of 'Auschwitz',[3] the inverted commas indicating a concept whose content remains beyond capture – that is, whose content remains absent. In many ways, much contemporary theorising from the side of absence has offered a radical version of Adorno's pessimistic work. Most notable in this stream are the writings of Lyotard[4] and Agamben.[5]

Alongside this shift of perspective is a radicalisation within the tradition of absence itself. Most notable is the hardening of Kant's connection between the trilogy of the absent ground of the moral law, the sublime, and the Second Commandment forbidding the representation of the 'Jewish God' (Kant,

---

1 E.g., see Gillian Rose's discussion of this debate in Rose, 1981, especially Chapter 1.
2 See note 4, Chapter 2.
3 Adorno, 1990; see, especially, Section III, 'Meditations on Metaphysics'.
4 See Lyotard, 1988, 1990 and 1993, Section IV, 'More "jews" '.
5 Agamben, 1999. See Chapters 2 and 4 of the present study.

2000, p 156) into a trilogy in which the Holocaust is its absent core. This chapter offers an engagement with this development through a discussion of Desmond Manderson's highly original and innovative article, 'From hunger to love: myths of the source, interpretation, and constitution of law in children's literature' (Manderson, 2003).

Drawing on the contrast between legal positivism and legal ethics, Manderson's reading of Maurice Sendak's classic children's story, *Where the Wild Things Are* (Sendak, 1991), offers a thesis that is grounded on the idea of the absence of ethics within modern law. This absence, he argues, is brought about by the dominance (and domination) of a legal positivism that emphasises obedience to the narrow meaning of the text at the expense of negotiation, responsibility and context. The first section of this essay argues that Manderson undermines his argument through reading positivism too positivistically, thereby breaching his own interdiction on ways of reading the law. I argue that this mistake arises from Manderson's appropriation of Adorno's 'immanent critique',[6] in which contradiction is substituted by absence. This first section is organised around the question of whether 'absence' can, like 'contradiction', be treated as *mediating* between legal positivism and legal ethics.

Assuming a negative answer to this question, a further question arises. If ethics is absent from rational cognition, such as positivism, by what means can its presence, first, become known and, second, become actualised? The answer to this question returns Manderson to an aestheticisation of law, of a 'legal ethics' that can only be intimated but never fully comprehended. I argue, finally, that this aestheticisation of law and the nature of its content express the continuing trope of the conflation of ethics, aesthetics and the Holocaust and its radical distinction from the trope of positivism, rationality and history; a result that indicates the contradiction of absence that lies buried within the absence of contradiction.

Immanent critique: the equivocation of positivism

Drawing on the work of HLA Hart and Hans Kelsen, Manderson offers an authoritarian and unidimensional picture of legal positivism in which obedience, certainty of meaning and injustice are brought together.

> The notion of obedience and the theory of hard-core meaning are necessarily connected. Obedience requires the following of rules without any reconsideration of them and, therefore, requires them to have some

---

6   Manderson, 2003, p 119.

> objective content that can be determined by the law-*giver*, alone and in advance. And Hart's lesson for a child like Max would be this: we expect you to learn the law, and to do so you would need only obey the words we tell you. On such an analysis, legal civility would be a function of one's obedience to the predetermined meaning of articulated norms.
>
> (Manderson, 2003, p 109)

At the heart of this representation of legal positivism is an emphasis upon the literalness of text and the presumed certainty of meaning at the expense of context and equivocality of meaning. More generally, these attributes contribute to conceiving of legal positivism as an arbitrary exercise of sovereign power into which all subjects are ensnared in an *a priori* constituted web. As a consequence, legal positivism is implicated in the perpetuation of injustice:

> The child's first encounter with law leaves him or her feeling, ironically, the sense of injustice. Children are 'before the law' in precisely the dual sense that Derrida draws out of Kafka's parable. That is, they are both ignorant of the legal order and yet subject to it. A child is a pre-legal subject and yet the quintessential object of regulation. Their lives are an experience of rules that are learned only through the process of breaking them.
>
> (Manderson, 2003, pp 106–7)

This view of positivism is contrasted with that of legal ethics. Reading the law ethically emphasises responsibility, equivocation, negotiation, taking into account the context of the words that acknowledge the slippage of meaning that is to be negotiated, respect for difference, honour for the law, in which law appears as third party, occupying the space between words and between persons:[12]

> A rule can never capture the complex process of judgement that must always be experienced as both bound and unbound, unique and universal. To be responsible is precisely to *respond* to the particularities of a situation and to make a choice in relation to it. Merely to apply in rote fashion the words of a rule is no exercise of responsibility at all, because it involves no decision at all; it is, in fact, to claim that one's hands are tied. No one would ask a machine or the wind to act *responsibly*. Obedience, then, is the polar opposite of responsibility. The recognition of difference, and the continually making judgements that attend to that difference, marks the end of the possibility of unquestioning obedience and the dawn of responsibility.
>
> (Manderson, 2003, p 123)

---

7 On this point, see also, Goodrich, 1996.

In characterising positivism as the 'polar opposite' of responsibility and reducing it to a species and justification of an unreflective, 'only obeying orders' obedience, Manderson overstates his case. He does so by elevating positivism's undoubtedly dominatory and authoritarian *tendencies* into its sole content. It is this closed and unequivocal reading of legal positivism that is set in opposition to something claimed (or posited) to exist outside or beyond itself – in this instance, legal ethics. In the discussion that follows, I argue that this strict bipolar reading of positivism and ethics emanates from Manderson's use of the critical tool of immanent critique, but in which Adorno's insistence upon contradiction is confused with that of absence.

Simon Jarvis identifies three aspects to Adorno's notion of immanent critique (Jarvis, 1998): first, identification of internal contradictions within the work itself; second, 'utopian negativity'; and, third, notions of 'the absolute'.

Internal contradictions

Jarvis explains the idea of internal contradiction as follows:

> 'Immanent' means remaining within. An immanent critique is one which 'remains within' what it criticises ... It uses the internal contradictions of a body of work to criticise that work in its own terms ... It is interested in what Adorno calls the 'truth-content' of entire works and authorships, which are more than the sum of its parts ... it is ... to understand the significance of the particular kinds of contradiction present in a given body of work – in particular, to understand what these contradictions tell us about the social experience out of which the work was written.
>
> (Jarvis, 1998, p 6)

At the core of this understanding of immanent critique is the idea that, in identifying contradictions within the work, one has identified contradictions within the social world. In other words, the text and its fault lines express and include within itself its social, political, ethical and cultural context.

There is little doubt that Manderson is correct to identify a particular constellation of contradictions present within the concept of 'law', contradictions that are expressed in the dichotomy of legal positivism and legal ethics. However, Manderson does not bring this logic of immanent critique to bear upon what are for him the now *distinct* notions of positivism and ethics. Instead, the 'relationship' of legal ethics to legal positivism is expressed through the negative language of absences. Legal ethics is presented as that which legal positivism does not contain, as opposed to each possessing elements of the other. This point is evidenced in the manner in which the characteristics of legal positivism and legal ethics are articulated through a series of oppositions rather than that of internal contradictions; a point illustrated through a brief discussion of text and context in the work of Hart and Kelsen.

One of the most relevant contexts of the writings of both of these thinkers is the rise of counter-liberal social and political tendencies that culminated in the racist totalitarianism of Nazi Germany. This context comes to the surface in Hart's depiction of legal positivism upon which Manderson relies. In this 1958 article for the *Harvard Law Review*, Hart was concerned with the difficult legacy of Nazi totalitarianism and the crimes committed in and under its name. It is a legacy, one needs add, that had remained relatively unexamined until that time and for many decades since.[8]

Correspondingly, it becomes obvious that a significant motivation for Kelsen's development of legal formalism (it is, in fact, questionable whether Kelsen can be called a legal 'positivist'[9]) was to oppose and neutralise contemporaneous theories of law and state founded upon historical and/or organic myths of *volk*. The irony of Kelsen's assertion of the autonomy of law is that it can be interpreted equally convincingly as political as well as legal work. It is in this way that the broader context (including ethics) of Kelsen's formalism attains visibility within the words of his texts. It is precisely this context that comes to be expressed *within* the *Grundnorm* itself in its attempt to distinguish law from its extra-legal genesis and thereby ensure a body politic premised on inclusion rather than upon racist exclusion.

Utopian negativity

This last point leads into the second aspect of immanent critique: utopian negativity.

> Adorno's utopian negativity ... works through immanent critique. It cannot provide a blueprint for what the good life would be like, but only examines what our 'damaged' life is like. It hopes to interpret this damaged life with sufficient attention and imagination to allow intimations of a possible, undamaged life to show through.
>
> (Jarvis, 1998, p 9)

Following Hegel and Marx, Adorno eschews outlining a future utopia, a future perfect world. Taking Hegel's ironic comment '*hic Rhodus, hic saltus*'

---

8 See Cotterrell, 2003, Chapter 5. See, also, Stolleis, 1998; Jacobson and Schlink, 2000; Georges and Ghaleigh, 2003.
9 For a discussion of this point, see Freeman, 2001, Chapter 5.

('here is Rhodes, jump here') (Hegel, 1991, p 21) seriously, Jarvis notes Adorno's insistence that 'the social theorist [can] not pretend that he or she [is] speaking from some place outside society' (Jarvis, 1998, p 9). Rather than draw up and impose a blueprint for the perfect society upon the world in which the injustice it sought to diffuse is reinstalled, Adorno insists[10] that the elements for the 'good life' are already actualised. In this way, therefore, Adorno is categorical that future freedom is not absent from the world as it is, but is fragmented and diffused throughout it, including, of course, throughout the domain of law. It is also necessary to note that this actuality of a potential utopia from within the confines of a 'damaged life', in which the actual is rational and the rational actual, does *not* rule out of court the exercise of the imagination (of non-instrumental rationality), but is rather dependent upon it.[11]

In the light of these comments, it is clear that both Hart's and Kelsen's work contain a moment of utopian negativity through which a better future can be imagined even if limited in its actualisation. This utopianism is that element of political and legal thought which includes the dream of a universal community mediated through the rule of law in which, and through which, each individual is respected as a person regardless of class, creed or the more pernicious category of 'race'; it imagines a community of stability and security in which individuals are able to flourish to their full potential.

The nature of this discussion of the work of positivism's and formalism's modern proponents is not simply to counter Manderson's negative reading with a positive one. Rather, is the suggestion that Adorno's notion of immanent critique points less to the absence of legal ethics within legal positivism, of context within text, and more to the idea of contradiction within and between them. This suggestion is reinforced through the third attribute of immanent critique discussed by Jarvis: the notion of 'the absolute'.

The absolute

Manderson's substitution of absence over contradiction emphasises Walter Benjamin's influence over Adorno (Benjamin, 2003).[12] This influence is clear in Adorno's belief in the dominance of abstract exchange-value over the specificities of use-value so that 'anything can be made to stand for absolutely anything else'.[13]

---

10 See Rose, 1993, 'Introduction'; Rose, 1996, 'Introduction'. See, also, Seymour, 2001 and 2004.
11 On this point, see Rose, 1978, especially Chapter 2.
12 See also Rose, 1978, pp 35–42; Jarvis, 1998, p 10.
13 See on this point, Adorno and Horkheimer, 2002.

> Any person, any object, any relationship can mean absolutely anything else. With this possibility a destructive, but just verdict is passed on the profane world: it is characterised as a world in which the detail is of no importance.
>
> (Jarvis, 1998, p 10)

Adorno shorns this influence of its spiritual and messianic aura. Whereas Benjamin argues that 'without a perspective outside this "context of guilt" or "natural history" '[14] the context cannot be 'interpreted', Adorno insists in remaining within the domain of 'damaged life'. For Adorno, 'the absolute' is less a deistic figure or intervention from 'beyond' as it is fragments of freedom, of moments of 'utopian negativity', already present in the world. The materiality of this fragmentary nature of 'the absolute' is evidenced through its existence as an expression of the fragmentary nature of freedom as it exists in a society and social relations organised around the diverse division of labour. For Adorno, therefore, the appearance of 'the absolute', of freedom, of emancipation, cannot be positively thought in theory until it is positively expressed in practice.

In this section it has been argued that the rupture between legal positivism and legal ethics emerges through Manderson breaching his own codes of reading, a code that is made overt in the following:

> My own reading of Sendak is not obedient to the text, but *responsive to its purposes*, just as the concept of law that the text suggests involves the child who reads it in a growing responsibility to the laws and the principles surrounding them, rather than a *mere formal obedience to them*.
>
> (Manderson, 2003, p 100; emphasis added)

Manderson's reading of legal positivism, therefore, takes it at its own face value; it accepts positivism's own claims and ambitions without being 'responsive to its purposes', purposes inherent within its texts. Manderson, in other words, reads positivism too positivistically.

With absence prioritised over contradiction, an unbridgeable gap cannot but appear between legal positivism and legal ethics, between text and context. It is the consequences of this rupture that are discussed in the following section, and which bring to the fore the intimately connected issue of the aestheticisation of 'legal ethics'.

---

14 For a discussion of Benjamin's meaning of the term 'natural history' and Adorno's adaptation of it, see Rose, 1978, Chapter 3, and Paddison, 1993, Chapter 2.

'I'll eat you up': consumption and aestheticisation

A further dimension of Manderson's thesis, in which Sendak uses the phrase 'I'll eat you up', compounds the difficulties associated with absence over contradiction. Drawing on the ethical philosophy of Emmanuel Levinas, Manderson offers a distinction between hunger and love, themes he sees as central to the nature of *Where the Wild Things Are*. On the one hand, there is love, which

> as a positive constitutive force is built upon the recognition of difference ... The very word *relationship* is integral to most understandings of love; it implies a connection between two bodies that maintain their distinctness.
>
> (Manderson, 2003, p 122)

On the other hand, there is hunger. In its consumption, hunger is said to absorb the other into the self, an absorption that destroys difference. It represents 'forms of narcissism that merely seek or reproduce sameness'.

> To say 'you are just like me' is a way of talking about me. Emmanuel Levinas explained this paradox through the experience of desire. The danger of desire is that it 'tends to bring the object "close enough" to be engulfed' by the self, and, consequently, destroys the sensation of difference that generated the attraction in the first place. Such desire, like a parasite, consumes the host that makes it possible. Love, for Levinas at least, if it is to survive, promises to respect difference and not obliterate it.
>
> (Manderson, 2003, p 122)

This depiction of hunger, desire and consumption as the erasure of difference echoes Adorno and Horkheimer's discussion of the fate of knowledge as the handmaiden of domination. Two facets of this connection are relevant here. First, the idea that what is not of 'use' in the sense of instrumental rationality is denied or expelled; it remains unrecognised. This 'non-rational' aspect remains 'outside' or 'beyond' the world moulded in the image of domination. Second, this consumption of object into concept is determined by the universality of exchange; that which remains outside the concept is what is left when all is made equal to everything else – particularity or difference – when all is made the same.

It is within this environment that positivism gains its meaning as that which circumscribes the contingency of the world to that of 'brute facts' (Jarvis, 1998, p 88) and invariable laws of nature. Reduced to a series of endless and inflexible repetitions, positivism converts its conceptual representation to 'given[s] before which thought must simply come to a halt ... positivism becomes the liquidation of the new, of the possibility that the facts might change'.[15] Positivism's domination manifests itself in its demands to obedience; demands, in other words, that the subject sacrifice its difference and particularity to the world as it is, to a world imbricated in domination and denial. Manderson himself draws a similar connection between legal positivism, consumption and domination.

> 'We'll eat you up – we love you so', say the wild things . . . neatly conflating hunger for another with love of them. But Max and his readers have already *understood on some instinctive level* that this consumption is an utterly terrifying threat: it is a perversion of love, the impossibility of any enduring community, and it augurs the annihilation of the child.
> (Manderson, 2003, p 122; emphasis added)

With the world consumed by the hunger and desire for instrumentality and its expression within positivistic concepts, both within and outside of law, a fundamental problem arises. What space remains that the 'absent-presence' of legal ethics can reach? This is a problem present in the contradiction inherent within Manderson's phrase 'understood on some instinctive level'. 'From hunger to love' points to two such spaces. The first space can be articulated as the 'jurisdiction of legal ethics' and, the second, as the 'jurisprudence of legal ethics'.

The jurisdiction of legal ethics

The jurisdiction of legal ethics draws on the familiar figure of the subject of legal positivism – an isolated monad, autonomous and independent, pursuing its own self-interest through which all others, and the social totality, is seen as a hindrance. This image is given a twist by Manderson in his emphasis upon this subject's absolute separation and subservience to the external sovereignty of the lawgiver, a sovereign that imposes its will upon this abject legal subject in such a way that the only obligation that inheres on the latter is that of automatic obedience.

It is precisely in the unrecognised and unacknowledged space that is erased by this positivistic concept of law that Manderson locates the jurisdiction of legal ethics. It is a space in which the sovereignty of law is said to be shared and its meaning negotiated. In it, law does not 'consume' the other, but acknowledges and develops difference and distinctiveness through that communication

---

15 It is interesting to note that in this account of positivism, Adorno comes perilously close to denying any dialectic between positivism and its 'remains', a problem that he solved, at least to a certain extent, through the triad of notion of identity, non-identity and rational-identity thinking (see Rose, 1978, Chapter 3).

and negotiation. Manderson argues that it is 'this [notion of law that] is meant by legal discourse: specific, embodied, interpretative practices' (Manderson, 2003, p 128).

Manderson explains this point through the illustration of the rituals of bedtime stories in which the parent 'reads to' the child. This account is sensitive especially to questions of power and hierarchy that exist in the parent and child relation, and the way in which such power can be neutralised or shared between the parties.

Manderson argues that the ownership of the reading materials, of the book, is shared between parent and child. This shared ownership manifests itself in the parent's possessing 'the key to the meaning of the book' and the child's physical custody of it. Interestingly, Manderson likens this dual notion of ownership to that of the trust.[16]

> The relationship of divided possession here is surprisingly complex and might well be summed up, both in legal and psychological terms, as a *trust*. The legal institution of the trust divided ownership in much this way, between the one who owns the physical form of something and the one entitled to benefit from the use of it. At the same time, only the social institution of trust between parent and child can reunite its physical form and the beneficial meaning it contains.
> (Manderson, 2003, p 129)

The upshot of this equitable relationship is that:

> The child is well aware of the double identity of the book, possessed by both and neither without the other; it gives them a sense of the necessity for co-operation and shared communication ... The constructive trust implicit in the act of reading demonstrates that the parent is already a 'collaborator and not a master'.
> (Manderson, 2003, pp 129–30)

With this distribution of possession over the unity of ownership, this dissolution of autonomy and isolation, the book and its meaning now become the object of shared conversation and negotiated meaning.

> Since the book itself is external to the direct relationship between parent and child, as if it were a third party, it presents the possibility of an interpretation in which both speaker and listener can participate.
> (Manderson, 2003, p 132)

---

16 For a less romantic reading of the trust, see Cotterrell, in Twining, 1986; *Lloyd's Bank plc v Rosset* [1991] 1 AC 107. For a discussion of the constructive trust in particular, see Diduck and Kaganas, 1999, pp 199, 202.

Opened in this way to the contingency of negotiation, the certainty of words claimed by legal positivism is undermined and replaced by meanings that can never be foreclosed.

> [T]he exegesis of the text is typically open-ended in its possibilities. Like Talmudic *mishnah*, the verses of a book like *Where the Wild Things Are* form the framework for a conversation: about the story, about Max's experience of the story, about the child's own and parallel experience.
> (Manderson, 2003, p 130)

Aside from the context of the reading situation and the readers' experience informing the meaning of the text to be negotiated, Manderson is emphatic in noting that:

> crucially, the text is not just a description of this cathartic event, but an occasion for the event itself, an invitation to a dialogue about feelings and experiences that both parent and child might share.
> (Manderson, 2003, p 120)

Taken together, these factors bring to the fore Manderson's central point: the way in which the sovereign authority of the positivistic text, its purported certainty of meaning and its in-built demand for obedience, is dislodged and supplanted by the openness of meaning brought about through the negotiation and communication of the parties. Informed as it is by their diverse and unique experiences, context informs text. It is this methodology of juridical interpretation that permits one and all to be responsible to, and to assume *responsibility for*, the law.

> The sparseness of both text and illustrations implies a secrecy that demands investigation. Like the *Mona Lisa*, a good children's book is inscrutable enough, to incite its own supplement ... The supplement is called forth by the form, it is the strength of the form ... But this approach is anything but a literal analysis of textual facts. This is the exercise of judgement that the child's reading mandates; the judgement that the text alone cannot hope to provide.
> (Manderson, 2003, p 131)

It is, in turn, such interpretative strategies that are said to bring the absence of ethics into presence, to make ethics resound in the words of the text itself.

> The skill of reading texts allows the unfolding of complex chains of events far into the future and long in the past. Without the ability to represent what is not present, without the capacity, therefore, to project

one's ideas into an absence, there can be no morality (the point is a familiar Kantian one).

(Manderson, 2003, p 121)

The jurisprudence of legal ethics

It is through this discussion of 'the jurisprudence of legal ethics' that the fault lines present in Manderson's reading of law come clearly into view.

As with its jurisdiction, the jurisprudence of legal ethics indicates something within the interstices, something 'outside' or 'beyond' the insular hermeneutics of legal positivism. This point is implied through Manderson's conflation of absence and externality. For example, toward the end of 'From hunger to love', he states:

> a contextual approach has already begun to pry apart the 'strict and complete legalism' of the very young child. The child is beginning to see that the 'why' of law and the 'what' of law are inextricably connected. This is what Fuller calls its 'external morality' and no system of interpretation can function without it.
>
> (Manderson, 2003, p 121)

Similarly, in an insightful comment on Derrida's 'Force of Law', Manderson notes the way in which *all* legal judgments are informed by a moment of externality.

> Whilst Hans Kelsen, therefore, would insist that only the *Grundnorm* – the first law of a community that establishes the conditions under which it takes place – suffers from this deficiency, Derrida argues that every norm contains within it a tiny fractal *Grundnorm* of its own, some decision or judgement that remains unmandated by the past.
>
> (Manderson, 2003, p 107)

This motif of absence as externality continues in Manderson's already noted attempt to externalise the ethical source of law. As custodians and negotiators of meaning of the book, the book now appears as a 'third party' over and above those from whom responsibility toward it is demanded. Paradoxically, whilst the interpreters are empowered through the praxis of legal ethics, they are correspondingly *disempowered* from the origination or founding of that source, of that text. The book, in other words, appears as a radicalised image of the positivist lawgiver admitting of an even greater distance between authorial and authoritative, command and subject.

This discussion of the jurisdiction and jurisprudence of legal ethics throws up immediate similarities with the nature of the jurisdiction and jurisprudence of Judaism. Although almost absent in Manderson's article itself, the connections and similarities between the two are indicated in Manderson's advocacy for an interpretative strategy akin to that of 'Talmudic *Mishnah*' (Manderson, 2003, p 132). This mode of reading, here equated with an ethics of reading, is alluded to also in the notion of 'supplementing' the bare words of a text. Such supplementing requires that words are pored over and endlessly debated in a spirit of collaboration (which, of course, does not negate hierarchy) leading to its relevance and application within contemporary contexts. What is *not* permitted, or what breaks these rules of interpretation, these rules of ethics, is the calling into question of the foundational status (and its authorship) of the *Torah*, the law itself. Replicating the power of the positivist sovereign, one is not permitted to call into question the text's own *Grundnorm*.

This connection between legal ethics and Judaism is further evidenced by Manderson's reference to the idea that the telling of the story is not just a description of past events, but 'an occasion for the event itself, an invitation to a dialogue about feelings and experiences that both parent and child might share' (Manderson, 2003, p 130). This notion of eternal presence replicates the Passover *Seder* edict to recount the story of the Exodus *as if* the participants at the table were themselves present at that event. This similarity between Manderson's ethical reading and the *Seder* is strengthened further by the idea that the narration of the story is such as to encourage questions, dialogue and interpretation. The jurisprudence of legal ethics appears, therefore, as the jurisprudence of Judaism, or, rather, a specifically 'post-Holocaust' notion of Judaism – of a 'Judaism without Jews'.

Ethics as Judaism without Jews: aestheticising the Holocaust

In his discussion of Levinas' distinction between hunger and love, Manderson notes that:

> love involves a gesture outside of oneself, and not just the grasping of things to convert them into *part* of oneself. Love is not just fuel; it must be a burning bush, alight but *un*consumed.
> (Manderson, 2003, p 122; emphasis in the original)

Manderson's use of the imagery of the burning bush, as that which burns but does not consume, brings to the fore the place and the meaning of the Holocaust implicitly contained within his thinking on legal ethics.

In its literal sense, a holocaust points to something (not necessarily, a sacrifice) consumed by fire. Yet, by making reference to the idea of that which is 'alight but unconsumed', Manderson is indicating that something remains after the conflagration; that something is left over once the desire of consumption has satiated itself. For Manderson, that remnant is Judaism, a

Judaism; in other words, without Jews that, as noted, becomes the model and meaning of legal ethics.

This notion of legal ethics as a Judaism without Jews returns us to Manderson's discussion of the nature of positivism. As noted, positivism is the conceptualisation of a world dominated in the name of instrumental rationality. Although variations remain as to specifics, the Jews came to be conceptualised as that which was surplus to requirements (Adorno[17] and Arendt[18]), as a difference that could not be universalised (Bauman[19]) or as an ethics that remained in 'Europe's' subconscious (Lyotard[20]). They were murdered, in other words, under the name of a concept, a concept of 'the Jews'.

As with all positivistic concepts, this concept of 'the Jews' is said to leave something unacknowledged and unrecognised; a something that continued and continues to be present even when the concept has been eradicated in a holocaust. And, as Manderson and others imply, this remnant is an ethical Judaism, or a Judaism of ethics, a Judaism and an ethics that remain within the interstices of the modern, rational, world.

This connection, or rather sublation, of legal ethics, the Holocaust and a Judaism without Jews is brought into closer view through their respective aestheticisation. As does legal ethics as a Judaism without Jews, the Holocaust comes to be presented as that which cannot be represented.[21] Concerned as it is with the absences within modernity in general and the absence of ethics in particular, the Holocaust escapes cognitive representation.[22] In the wake of this failure of representation, an understanding of the Holocaust, like the understanding of legal ethics, is replaced by its aestheticisation. It becomes the limit of human knowledge and human cognition. In so doing, legal ethics, Judaism without Jews and the Holocaust take on the aura of positivism, of 'given events', 'before which thought must simply come to a halt'.

'Outside' or 'beyond' human cognition, the Holocaust takes on extra-human dimensions. Like legal ethics and Judaism, it becomes something whose origins are so mysterious[23] that, as much as we can negotiate its meaning and speak of it as if we were there, we can never begin to *understand* and so represent it through our critical faculties. Rather, this 'three in one'

---

17 See Adorno and Horkheimer, 2002.
18 See Arendt, 1979.
19 See Bauman, 1991. See also Chapter 2 above.
20 See Lyotard, 1990 and 1993c. See also Chapter 4.
21 See Adorno, 1990, and Lyotard's radicalisation of Adorno's thought in Lyotard, 1988.
22 In some instances, it is precisely these 'modern' modes of cognition that are held *responsible* for the Holocaust; see Bauman, 1991, and James MacMillan's attempt to bring into being a 'spiritual modernism' (MacMillan, 2003).
23 On this point, see Lyotard, 1990 and 1993.

becomes that which throws these faculties into disarray, a disarray that is said to act as a constant reminder of humanity's own hubris.

It is in this aestheticised form that the Holocaust comes to be presented as the absent 'context' of modernity, its instrumentality, its positivism and its concepts. It comes to occupy the void that, since Kant, has been said to haunt the modern world. Taking on the characteristics of the moral law, it shares with it the inability of representation. As something 'sublime' it remains faithful to the prohibition of the second commandment. 'Perhaps sensed' or 'understood on an instinctive level', it becomes the law according to which we must act *as if* we were cognisant of it, and incumbent upon us in living our lives as if it were eternally occurring. And, in a final paradox, the Holocaust becomes as much the context for Manderson's legal ethics as I argued it was for both Kelsen's and Hart's positivism.

Conclusion

Manderson's conflation and aestheticisation of legal ethics, Judaism without Jews and the Holocaust on the one hand, and its radical separation and opposition to legal positivism on the other hand, is, I have argued, the result of his substitution of absence for contradiction in the utilisation of Adorno's immanent critique. As a consequence, Manderson is unable to acknowledge or recognise the implication and imbrication of each within the other. In place of contradiction that emphasises and mediates the ethics of positivism and the positivism of ethics, absence cannot mediate, it can only obliterate.

It is for these reasons that Manderson's thinking offers a series of radical separations and oppositions – those between ethics and positivism, text and context, aesthetics and politics, modernity and Judaism, Jews and Judaism; oppositions that Manderson lay at the feet of positivism. This paradox of replication exhausts itself in the fact that in the opposition between positivism and aesthetics, legal ethics, Judaism and the Holocaust become imbued with the same characteristics Manderson identified with positivism in general. Removed from the ambit of human activity and human cognition, they confront the world with the power and mystery of a natural force. Outside or beyond the scope of human possibility, they demand of humanity its subjection and adoption and in this way ethics, like positivism, inverts into domination, and the Holocaust into mythology.

Chapter 4

Antisemitism and emancipation: the *ressentiment* of loss

> EP Thompson draws our attention to how far the structure of *Capital* is dominated by the categories of its antagonist.
>
> (Fine, 2001, p 87)

One of the markers of critical accounts of antisemitism and the Holocaust is their location within the context and praxis of modern emancipation as it is manifested socially, politically and juridically. In this essay, I offer an examination of four works that illustrate this location: Nietzsche, Sartre, Lyotard and Agamben. This choice is far from arbitrary. Without in any way diminishing their differences and distinctions, underpinning them all is a common idea: antisemitism arises from a *ressentiment* brought into being through the presence of an ontological loss or absence. This loss or absence is, in turn, treated as being inherent within the very praxis of modern emancipation. For Nietzsche, that loss is of an inherent human freedom; for Sartre, it is the loss of community; for Lyotard, it is the loss of 'the ethical'; whilst, for Agamben, it is the loss of 'the natural' or the 'mystery' of life and of birth.

Another theme that connects these thinkers is the manner in which their accounts, despite their seemingly anti-antisemitic intentions, replicate many of the tenets of the antisemitic worldview. This unintentional collusion appears in three ways. The first is an increasing tendency to treat modern emancipation as doomed to failure and as a risk not worth taking. This belief is intimately connected to the second point of commonality: that there is an ontological element within individuals or groups that makes them immune to changes brought about at the level of society; a society that, in turn, is presented as an 'artifice' built over a 'naturalness'.

The consequence of these tendencies leads to the third element of their replication of antisemitism. The assumed failure of emancipation and artificiality of society brings a fatalism that manifests itself in a sense of powerlessness leading to a *ressentiment* against not only the emancipated world as it is, but against the very idea of emancipation.

It is the combination of these themes that creates what I call 'Holocaust dissolution'. Holocaust dissolution is the worrying theoretical trend in which critiques of antisemitism and the Holocaust are submerged within a generalised critique of emancipation itself. Holocaust dissolution is worrying because its undoubtedly unintentional consequence is the inauguration of a new loss and a new *ressentiment*, this time not targeted against the Jews directly, but rather against antisemitism and the Holocaust.

Nietzsche: antisemitism as breach of contract

Nietzsche's most considered reflections on the perniciousness of antisemitism in his times appears in *On the Genealogy of Morals*. This work was written some 15 years after the Jews of Germany had been granted full and (seemingly) final political and civil emancipation. It was also the same time as the concept of 'antisemitism' had entered the political and social lexicon. This antisemitism pointed in two distinct, but interrelated, directions. First, the emancipation of Jews through abstract and formal rights was merely a sham masking the Jews' 'true' and 'immutable' essence through which, and this is the second element, they could not but seek to and succeed in undermining an equally natural Germanic presence. Indeed, for the young Nietzsche, as for all antisemites, the artifice of society was nothing other than a means the Jews devised for such a battle.

Perhaps it is because of this closeness to the antisemitism of his time[1] that Nietzsche was the first thinker to acknowledge the full potential of what was then a uniquely novel phenomenon. His reflections on this ideology are breathtaking for the manner in which they capture its modernity, its repugnance, its radicalism and its mythology of freedom that allowed it to be presented by Duhring, amongst others, as a movement of 'the left'.[2] In ways that seem to prefigure Hannah Arendt's ideas on the question of antisemitism and emancipation,[3] Nietzsche indicates the manner in which antisemitism both grows out of existing conditions which simultaneously threaten them with extinction.

One of the most significant aspects of Nietzsche's account of antisemitism is its presentation as a moral as opposed to a social or political phenomenon. However, it is this latter aspect that, I believe, can be brought into question. In the discussion that follows, I argue that the underlying structure of Nietzsche's understanding of antisemitism and its connection with modern emancipation is that of the contract and associated terms of exchange and equivalence. It is for this reason that Nietzsche's critique of the genealogy of

---

1   His relationship with Wagner is particularly telling on the point (see Safranski, 2002).
2   On this point, it is interesting to note that, at least in the *Genealogy*, if not *Birth of Tragedy*, Nietzsche's unremitting target is not the nationalism of Bismarkian Germany, but the 'left' socialism of Eugen Duhring.
3   See Chapters 6 and 7.

morality, as well as the place of antisemitism within it, can be read as a critique of both the natural law of the social contract and the positivism of the legal subject of a civil society organised around the exchange of private property. It is this contractual form of Nietzsche's account of antisemitism that links it so accurately to the society in which and through which it is produced and which, in turn, is the reason for its implied rejection in the face of an asocial and ahistorical anti-Jewish hostility.

In bringing these points to the fore, I identify and follow several 'layers' of exchange that Nietzsche's genealogy uncovers[4] within the praxis of modern morality. I argue that, for Nietzsche, each of these layers can be related to each other through the common aim of masking, rationalising and compensating for an original and originating loss: a loss of freedom that lies at the very heart and meaning of emancipation. It is this initial exchange that founds all later moments of exchange and the sense of unease or discomfort ('bad conscience') that Nietzsche believes arises from it. The paradox for Nietzsche is that, far from relieving this discomfort, each exchange results in a deepening of the initial, ontological situation out of which this bad conscience turns into *ressentiment* and through which antisemitism enters the modern world. It is, however, only with a final fateful exchange, through which the man of *ressentiment*, Nietzsche's slave, seeks to exchange *himself* for that of the noble that antisemitism breaks free from its constraints and offers the potential to reduce society to ashes. With acute awareness, in describing his own time, Nietzsche may well have identified a *possible* future, but he should not be treated as prophesising what actually came to pass. To believe otherwise is to believe that the Holocaust was itself ontologically determined.

The first and most fundamental moment of exchange accompanies the exchange of freedom for emancipation into society. It is here that the 'bad conscience' that is to form the ground of *ressentiment* and antisemitism comes into existence. The bad conscience arises when the 'natural' attributes of the noble are denied, repressed and turned back against the individuals themselves.

Nietzsche makes it clear that the necessity for such denial and repression is the production of the 'Sovereign Individual' – the person with 'the right to make promises' (Nietzsche, 2002, II: 2). In place of the spontaneity, vitality, physicality and cruelty of the free being are those of temporality, rationality, responsibility and discipline; the very attributes needed to enter into and honour contracts – promises made in the past that commits one to the future. The cost of this exchange, however, is dramatic and traumatic. The attributes

---

4 For discussions of Nietzsche's concept of 'genealogy', see Foucault, 'Nietzsche, genealogy, history', in Richardson, 2001. See also Blondel, 'The question of genealogy' and Conway, 'Genealogy and critical method', in Schacht, 1994.

of the noble that outside society was visited on others (and, it should be a noted, with a good, or free, conscience), now changes direction and turns on the 'sovereign' himself. It is this development that gives rise to an ontological sense of unease and discomfort, as well as its importance for the world as a whole. It is necessary to quote Nietzsche at length on this point.

> I look on the bad conscience as a serious illness to which man was forced to succumb by the pressure of the most fundamental of all changes which he experienced, – that change whereby he finally found himself imprisoned within the confines of society and peace . . . the poor things were reduced to relying on thinking, inference, calculation, and the connecting of cause and effect, that is, on relying on their 'consciousness' . . . I do not think that there has been such a feeling on earth, such a leaden discomfort, – and, meanwhile, the old instincts had not suddenly ceased to make their demands! But it was difficult and seldom possible to give in to them: they mainly had to seek new and as it were underground satisfactions. All instincts which are not discharged outwardly *turn inwards* – this is what I call the *internalization* of man . . . These terrible bulwarks with which state organisations protected themselves against the old instincts of freedom . . . had the result that all those instincts of the wild, free, roving man were turned backwards, *against man himself*. Animosity, cruelty, the pleasure of pursuing, raiding, changing and destroying – all this was pitted against the person who had such instincts: *that* is the origin of the 'bad conscience'.
>
> (Nietzsche, 2002, II:16)

It is in this way that Nietzsche brings together the trajectory of emancipation with the trajectory of the bad conscience; to understand the one is to understand the other.

As powerful as the attributes that it refuses, it is questionable whether, of itself, the person could survive such discomfort. From the outset then society contains within it the seeds of its own destruction. That society did not destroy itself immediately is down to the fact that the discomfort brought about by the bad conscience was given a meaning and a purpose. As Nietzsche argues, it is not suffering *per se* that runs the risk of destroying the person, it is the idea of suffering *without purpose* (Nietzsche, 2002, III: 28). Here is the second moment of exchange: the valuelessness of life lived in society was exchanged for a life given an ideal or, in Nietzsche's terms, a *moral* value. As with the process of exchange itself, the 'use-value' of social existence is coming to be replaced by an 'exchange-value', as its meaning comes to be seen in moral terms.

It is important to realise that morality does not *relieve* the bad conscience, but, rather, offers it a meaning and justification. In breaking with the moralists of his day, Nietzsche traces this content of meaning to the contractual relationships of exchange. Suffering came to be given a moral significance through an idea of a guilt arising from the sense of being in debt. Not only was suffering given a meaning in this way, but the degree to which one suffered was not arbitrary. Premised upon the model of the contract and of exchange, the amount one suffered was equivalent to the amount one was in debt.

> Have these genealogists of morality up to now ever remotely dreamt that, for example, the main moral concept '*Schuld*' ('*guilt*') descends from the material concept of '*Schulden*' ('*debts*') . . . And where did this primeval, deeply-rooted and perhaps now ineradicable idea gain its power, this idea of equivalence between injury and pain? . . . in the contractual relationship between *creditor* and *debtor*, which is as old as the very conception of a 'legal subject' and itself refers back to the basic forms of buying, selling, trade and traffic.
>
> (Nietzsche, 2002, II:4)

That this sense of guilt for an unpaid debt should be so strong a ground for the entire edifice upon which the genealogy of morality is built turns again on the nature of the modern legal subject as 'the one with the right to make promises'. So strong was this necessity that the obligation and responsibility to honour one's agreements, no matter what the intervening state of affairs might be, came to be the very meaning of 'conscience' itself. It is for this reason, therefore, that the ontologically originating bad conscience should come to adopt a legal form of debt and guilt for non-payment.

Whilst the moral significance and content of the bad conscience has deepened through its imbrication with the legal, contractual form, it has still not 'matured' into *ressentiment*. Although the unease that accompanies emancipation is presented in terms of debt and guilt, there is, as yet, nothing to indicate that the debt cannot be repaid; that the suffering rationalised in this manner can be brought to an end. However, this hope and potential for redemption, for the debt to be repaid, ends with the death of Christ.[5]

It is with this development that Nietzsche introduces a third moment, or layer, of exchange. Drawing on the anthropology of his time, Nietzsche notes that the more successful an individual or society becomes, the more one feels one owes one's ancestors; or, in other words, the more one feels in debt to the past and the more one feels one owes to a creditor. This process, Nietzsche argues, culminates in the relationship of increasing success being met with the

---

5 That Nietzsche appears to be offering a chronology of morality is only partially the case. The notion of *genealogy* not only points to 'hidden' layers, but also to the way the past is seen from the present.

idea of an absolute debt, of a debt owed but for which any and all payment is impossible. This sense of irredeemable debt – and, eternal *guilt* – reaches its apotheosis with the interpretation of Christ's death as the creditor dying for the sake of His debtors.

> And could anyone . . . using all the ingenuity of the intellect, think up a more *dangerous* bait? Something to equal the enticing, intoxicating, benumbing, corrupting power of that symbol of the 'holy cross', to equal the horrible paradox of a 'God on the Cross', to equal that mystery of an unthinkable final act of extreme cruelty and self-crucifixion of God for the *salvation of mankind*.
>
> (Nietzsche, 2002, I:8)

It is in this presentation of Christ's death that any means and any possibility of expiation is terminated for good.

What distinguishes this moment of exchange, of course, is the coming into existence of a debt that can never be repaid and that *can never* alleviate the sense of guilt that accompanied all relations of credit and debt. The paradox of Christ's death, and one that Nietzsche does not hesitate to emphasise, is that whilst, on the one hand, Christ's death is said to offer redemption for 'original guilt' or 'original sin', it simultaneously draws the sense of guilt to unparalleled and unheralded depths.

The consequences of this impossible contract are spelt out explicitly.

> Now these concepts 'guilt' and 'duty' *are to be* reversed – but against *whom*? It is indisputable; firstly against the 'debtor', in whom the bad conscience now so firmly establishes itself, eating into him, broadening out and growing, like a polyp, so wide and deep that in the end, with the impossibility of expiating the guilt, is conceived the impossibility of discharging the penance, the idea that it cannot be paid off.
>
> (Nietzsche, 2002, II:21)

Powerless in the face of this irredeemable debt and suffering unbearable and unexpiatable guilt, the 'debtor' looks for ways and means to escape from such self-inflicted torture. One such means, and the one to come to hand most readily, is to look around for someone *else* to blame and to hold responsible and, in so doing, relieve their pain. Yet, as Nietzsche notes, the very essence of *ressentiment* is an inability to act, in this instance an inability that is itself a product of the guilt and impotence they feel in the face of their debt. In exchange for the impossibility of acting, they come together as a 'herd', and feed themselves on a diet of imagined harms and imagined revenge. Nietzsche describes the condition of this herd with the recondite skill of a medieval artist depicting hell.

> The sufferers, one and all, are frighteningly willing and inventive in their pretexts for painful emotions; they even enjoy being mistrustful and dwelling on wrongs and imagined slights: they rummage through the bowels of the past and present for obscure, questionable stories which will allow them to wallow in tortured suspicion, and intoxicate themselves and their own poisonous wickedness – they rip open the oldest wounds and make themselves bleed to death from scars long since healed, they make evil-doers out of friend, wife, child and anyone else near them. 'I suffer: someone or other must be guilty' – and every sick sheep thinks the same.
> (Nietzsche, 2002, III:15)

Such is the state of those 'Sovereign Individuals', of those whose contractual responsibilities have brought them to this condition, when Nietzsche introduces the figure of the 'Ascetic Priest', the equivocal figure through which living becomes 'interesting'. It is with his intervention that:

> [The] slaves' revolt in morality turns creative and gives birth to values: the *ressentiment* of those who, being denied the proper response of action compensate for it only with imaginary revenge.
> (Nietzsche, 2002, I:10)

This moment of creativity, it is to be noted, is not the *dispersion* of *ressentiment*, but its *redirection*, its containment within the herd.

> But [the herd's] shepherd, the ascetic priest, says to [the man of *ressentiment*], 'Quite right, my sheep! Somebody is to blame, but you yourself are this somebody, you yourself alone are to blame for it, *you yourself are to blame for yourself* . . . This is bold enough, wrong enough: but at least one thing has been achieved by it, the direction of *ressentiment* is . . . changed.
> (Nietzsche, 2002, III:15)

In effect, what the Ascetic Priest has achieved is nothing more nor less than a renegotiation of the initial terms of the contract. With the disappearance of the creditor along with any possibility of repaying the debt to him, the possibility of expiation lies in the hands of the debtor himself. If he is unable to redeem the debt, it is, so the Ascetic Priest tells him, because of *his* guilt, of *his* inability to meet the stringent demands placed upon him by the demands of asceticism.

Accompanying this renegotiation of the contract is a corresponding revaluation of its substance: the meaning of life itself, or, rather, the meaning of the existence of 'the bad conscience' that is endemic within emancipation. With the advent of asceticism, life and living lost all value in itself and instead became meaningful as a means to a further and endlessly deferred goal, the cancellation of a debt. In other terms, and in keeping with the nature of value prevalent in an exchange society, the value of life brought into being by asceticism is that of the dominance of exchange-value over use-value. Asceticism introduces the idea of exchanging a life meaningless in itself (as something to be consumed for what it is) for a future life of *meaning*, one in which one can and does repay the debtor for his sacrifice and promise. It is here, therefore, that Nietzsche's ambivalent attitude to the Ascetic Priest arises. It is this ambivalence that is present in his comment that:

> Priests make *everything* more dangerous, not just medicaments and healing arts but pride, revenge, acumen, debauchery, love, lust for power, virtue, sickness; – in any case, with some justification one could add that man first became an *interesting animal* on the foundation of this *essentially dangerous* form of human existence, the priest, and the human soul became *deep* in the higher sense and turned *evil* for the first time – and, of course, these are the two basic forms of man's superiority, hitherto, over other animals.
>
> (Nietzsche, 2002, 1:6)

In keeping with Nietzsche's genealogical approach to morality, it is important to note that for Nietzsche asceticism and its values do not come to an end with the advent of secularism. It is in terms of the idea that the present is but the means to a future end, an idea he sees as the heart of modern philosophy from Kant onward, that he sees asceticism as an active presence within modern emancipated society.

Crucially, however, Nietzsche is at pains to emphasise that this renegotiating and revaluing of life and its conditions does not 'cure' the sufferer, the man of *ressentiment*. (Indeed, for Nietzsche, the very idea of a 'cure' that leaves society in place is impossible, since, masked under, and providing the impetus for all these layers of exchange is precisely the ontological loss of freedom that is the essence of emancipation itself). Instead, the ascetic priest, in both its religious and secular form, inflames both the conditions of the agreement as well as the reward promised. However, this gambit of simultaneously turning up the heat under the boiling cauldron of *ressentiment*, whilst keeping the lid firmly in place, is a dangerous, risk-filled endeavour. At any moment there is the possibility of the venom of *ressentiment* boiling over the top and spilling out in all directions. It is, moreover, a possibility that Nietzsche identifies with the existence within emancipation of antisemitism in general and the poisonous rhetoric of Eugen Duhring in particular.[6]

---

6 It is interesting to note that Nietzsche locates this discussion immediately following the discussion of the climax of legal relations where law ends in mercy as a form of 'forgetting' harms committed because it is so secure in its feeling of security. Moreover, in placing his criticism of Duhring here as well, Nietzsche offers a strong defence of law, before examining its negative effects through an account of the development of the 'bad conscience'.

What disgusts Nietzsche most about Duhring and his ilk and deserves his contempt like no other is his complete and utter inability to keep his word; to live up to the standards imposed on him by the terms of the 'new' contract. In keeping with his equivocal valuation of *ressentiment*, Nietzsche is well aware of the hardships and difficulties of leading an 'ascetic life'. He is aware, in other words, of the strength of character needed for a life that demands rationality, responsibility and discipline of which the privilege of 'the right to make promises' is the end result; of the strength of character to keep to the terms of a contract despite the vicissitudes of life; as well as the strength of character needed for a life of endless deferral in exchange for a deferred end.

Nowhere does this distinction between the immediacy of the antisemite and the mediacy of society, come into greater relief than in the respective meanings of 'justice'. The first is disinterested justice mediated by objective principles of exchange and equivalence; in other words, the justice of the contract.

> Just cast your eye around in history; in what sphere, up till now, has the whole treatment of justice, and the actual need for justice, resided? With men who react, perhaps? Not in the least: but with the active, the strong, the spontaneous and the aggressive. Historically, speaking, justice on earth presents – I say this [against Duhring] (who himself once confessed: 'The doctrine of revenge has woven its way through all my work and activities as the red thread of justice') – the battle, then, *against* reactive sentiment, the war waged against the same on the part of active and aggressive forces, which have partly expended their strength in trying to put a stop to the spread of reactive pathos, to keep it in check and within bounds, and to force some kind of compromise with it. Everywhere that justice is practised and maintained, the stronger power can be seen looking for means of putting an end to the senseless ravages of *ressentiment* amongst those inferior to it (whether groups or individuals), partly by lifting the object of *ressentiment* out of the hands of revenge, partly by substituting for revenge, a struggle against the enemies of peace and order, partly be working out compensation, suggesting, sometimes enforcing it, and partly by promoting certain equivalences for wrongs into a norm which *ressentiment*, from now on, has to take into account.
> (Nietzsche, 2002)

It is this sense of justice that the man of *ressentiment*, the antisemite, wants to exchange for a concept of justice the content of which is the immediacy of *revenge*.

> And, just as like comes to like, it will come as no surprise to find attempts coming once more to these circles [of 'antisemites and anarchists'], as so often before . . . to sanctify *revenge* with the term *justice* – as though

justice were fundamentally simply a further development of the feeling of having been wronged – and belatedly to legitimize with revenge emotional *reactions* in general, one and all.

(Nietzsche, 2002, II:11)

It is of the utmost importance to realise that these two perceptions of justice are *both* expressions of *ressentiment*. They are not to be understood as manifesting the 'character traits' of the noble and slave respectively. The former concept of justice grounds itself in the values of exchange, measure and context; of discipline, patience and mediation. The latter demands immediate action, unmediated by any values other than that of a revenge whose only limit is that of the harm suffered. Since, however, that harm is deep-seated and unbearable, so too will revenge take on such terrible dimensions.

As we have seen, it is, for Nietzsche, in the nature of *ressentiment* freed from the constraint of asceticism to look around for some one or some group to blame for the suffering they now feel, a suffering brought by the sense of an unpaid and unpayable debt. The others upon which the released venom of *ressentiment* splatters is that of the Jews, or rather that of the distorted image of 'the Jews'.

The Jews against whom the man of *ressentiment* wants revenge is, in fact, a product of the antisemite's imagination. He is the product of slave morality through which the 'other', against whom the slave measures and values himself, appears in grotesque and distorted terms. In an element of *ressentiment* that Nietzsche does not bring into relief, but is nonetheless present, the entire complexities of the social world, its paradoxes and contradictions, are reduced to and contained within one single and singular malevolent idea – the Jews. For the antisemite, this *idée fixée* of 'the Jew' is the answer given to any and all the causes of the suffering the man of *ressentiment* undoubtedly feels.

The deeper the feeling of suffering, therefore, the more it is said the Jews are going to be made to pay. In their conspiracies and machinations through which the Jews become endowed with omnipotent power, the slave imagines himself as nothing less that the noble the Jews have laid low through their 'Jewish means'.[7] The revenge they seek, therefore, is total and absolute; it is the revenge of the 'nobles', caught and trapped into the domesticity of society, and for the pain such confinement brought with it. Through the violence and barbarity of the immediacy of revenge, not only does he believe that the debt be repaid, and repaid with interest, but the means of such nihilism is nothing other than an apparent return or resurrection of the natural instincts that defined pre-social nobility. It is here, therefore, in the *means* of payment that a final moment of exchange appears, that of the slave *masquerading* as the noble. It is for this reason, therefore, that the declaration of war against the Jews is, at one and the same time, a declaration of war against society and

---

7 See Chapter 5.

its values; a war that makes even the possibility of any further exchange impossible.

Although Nietzsche's account of antisemitism rests upon a moral schema modelled upon the nature of contemporaneous society – that is, the realm of the exchange of private property – its roots and origins are said to lie elsewhere. Working backwards, so to speak, the first externality points to antisemitism's development and ultimate expression within the idealism of morality. Morality, in turn, came into existence as a means to rationalise a sense of suffering that accompanied life in society; this suffering that came about through an original and originating loss. That loss is of a pre-social, original freedom; the loss of freedom of natural instincts and natural hierarchy (of the values 'good' and 'bad'). The *ressentiment* that expresses itself through antisemitism is, in other words, a *ressentiment* against social life itself. Paradoxically, it is a *ressentiment* that Nietzsche shared with those he opposed wholeheartedly, but which, nonetheless, infuses his account of the connection between emancipation and antisemitism. It is this shared outlook that allows Nietzsche's account to be presented less as a sociology of antisemitism, but more an ontology of society, of which antisemitism is treated as a potential by-product, and which informs the following points.

First, that the causes of antisemitism are removed from the realm of social relations, a realm in which Jews live and act, to that of the idealism of morality in which the Jews appear solely through the (distorting) vision of the putative or potential antisemite. It is this absence of Jews that forms part of the antisemitic worldview and which is reproduced, for converse reasons, in Nietzsche's critical account. Second, and obviously related to this first point, is the idea that hostility to Jews is a product of the antisemite's own difficulties of living within society. Nietzsche's account of antisemitism, in other words, has little to say either about the nature of emancipated society, nor about the role of Jews in the emergence of this phenomenon.

Arising from these points is a third: that, as with the antisemite, if not the man of *ressentiment* in general, emancipation is perceived as an artifice built over and repressing a formerly 'natural' world in which everything had a place and there was a place for everything. The *ressentiment* that lies at the heart of antisemitism, in other words, is a consequence of the hubristic urge to create a new way of living. It follows from this point that Nietzsche, like those he is challenging, is pessimistic about the possibility of a society premised upon notions of egality and equality.

Despite these correlations between Nietzsche's critical engagement and the antisemitism he was confronting and opposing, Nietzsche's attitude to emancipation was equivocal. Unlike the antisemite, Nietzsche recognised the 'improvement' in humanity brought about by confinement in society and the moral teachings that accompanied it. It was as a consequence of this equivocality that Nietzsche was unequivocal about the futility and danger of attempts at turning back the clock, of a supposed return to a noble era, which he saw as nothing but an exercise in unrestrained *ressentiment*. Likewise, whilst he recognised antisemitism as a presence within society, he was far from equating hostility to the Jews with emancipation itself. In other words, despite his prescience in identifying antisemitism, there is nothing in Nietzsche's account of antisemitism that should be seen as heralding future events as a foregone conclusion.

Sartre, emancipation and antisemitism: between rights and *ressentiment*

Sartre's most sustained engagement with antisemitism is contained in the slim volume, *Anti-Semite and Jew*. Written in the autumn of 1944 and published in Paris in 1946 and the United States in 1948,[8] Sartre not only sought to understand antisemitism,[9] but also to remind a triumphant France of the specificity of the situation of the French Jews, of what Judaken calls 'the forgotten'.[10]

Sartre's account can be outlined briefly. Antisemitism arises through a *ressentiment* against the loss perceived to inhere within modern political emancipation – in this context, a loss of community. This *ressentiment* is redirected toward the Jews, or, rather, toward an image of 'the Jew' created by the antisemite.

Like Nietzsche, Sartre's account of antisemitism adopts an equivocal position. On the one hand, he seems to argue that the loss or absence of community that brings antisemitism into existence is nothing other than the product of the (distorted) imagination of the antisemite. On the other hand, there are times, especially in his more overtly normative statements, that this loss is an 'objective' fact. This initial equivocality echoes throughout his analysis and resurfaces not only in his discussion of the concept of 'the Jews', but also in his own *ressentiment* against what he sees as the shortcomings of emancipation.

Regardless of his own equivocality, Sartre's starting point is the idea that modern emancipation creates a civil society bereft of community or communality. Drawing heavily on Marx's critique of political emancipation in *On the Jewish Question*, Sartre paints a picture of modern society as comprising formally equal, abstract and autonomous owners of private property whose only contact with others is through the process of exchange mediated through

---

8 For the history of its publication and reception, see Rybalka, 1999.
9 Many of the criticisms leveled against *Anti-Semite and Jew* turn on the idea that, in writing this work, Sartre did not take cognisance of the fact of the death camps and, as such, explained more the antisemitism of the pogrom than the Holocaust (see Tenzo, 1999, for the most unforgiving position). It seems to me, however, less a problem of cognition, but more of a limitation of theory; that Sartre did not have the theoretical *imagination* within which to confront the extreme novelty of the exterminations.
10 Judaken, 2006, pp 123–8.

legal forms of rights and contract. Understood in this way, all persons are islands unto themselves.

Subjectively, this situation results in a grave and unending sense of instability and insecurity. Sartre argues that the bourgeois individual experiences a profound feeling of isolation. These individuals, he argues, are constantly and irretrievably weighed down by a sense of personal and unavoidable responsibility. These feelings are a consequence of their belief that their successes (but, more often, their failures) are a matter of *personal* (as opposed to social) responsibility. It is as a reaction to this situation that these individuals 'choose themselves' as antisemites. It is in their very opposition to 'the Jews' that the antisemites can begin to imagine themselves a member of a collectivity, one produced by what amounts to an example of the *ressentiment* of a slave morality.

Sartre is insistent that this subjective 'choice' to become an antisemite is never direct, but always mediated through one's ('objective') class position. It is as a consequence of this belief that Sartre believes such a choice is open only to members of the middle class. His argument here is that, unlike the position of the working class whose relationship to the means of production gives rise to an understanding of historical development as the movement of 'objective laws', the middle class attributes social attributes and developments to *human* forces, since, in terms that recall Adorno's description, this 'non-productive' realm is defined by the lure of human nuances.

It is as a consequence of this class-determined perspective that the middle class sees the world through the notion of different categories of human groups, each attributed its own alleged, particularistic, 'essence'. Driven by *ressentiment*, the antisemite measures his own 'innocence' for the world as it is, and the loss it incorporates, only after reference to the 'essential evil' of 'the Jews'. Through the prism of their class position, the antisemites appear to themselves to have re-ordered the world in a Manichean struggle between 'good' and 'evil'. By forming themselves, at least at the level of ideas and ideals, into a collectivity[11] through a *reaction* against another, hostile, community, the sense of uncertainty and instability appears to have been overcome.

This apparent and idealist overcoming of the *social* causes of their discomfort and *ressentiment* rests upon a further series of negative evaluations that stems from that of antisemite ('good') and Jew ('evil'). The first and most fundamental is the opposition between the 'social' and the 'natural'. In imagining a community absent of Jews, the antisemite postulates a mythical romantic connection to the soil. As a species of what Sartre terms 'primitive possession' (1995, p 23), this organic rootedness to the land trumps and withstands the artifice of claims premised upon abstract notions of private

---

11 This connection to *ressentiment* is illustrated by Sartre's reference to antisemites as a 'herd'.

property and legal-rational means of ownership. The value of such imaginings is that, unlike modern notions of private property – inherent within which is the idea that it is accessible to all through the sheer graft of personal will and personal effort – 'primitive possession' is inherently, *naturally*, limited only to those with the requisite links to the 'historical [that is, national] community' (1995, pp 79ff).

The symmetry between devaluation and revaluation is not exhausted through reference to the land or soil. Sartre argues that *all* objects come to be endowed with this alternative, intangible, mythical, irrational value that emanates from this 'nation'. The Jew – and, Sartre notes, the antisemite is the first to admit this fact – can own objects *legally* and understand them *rationally*, but can never *truly* possess them or appreciate them for what they '*really*' are.

Sartre notes that, from the perspective of the antisemite, as soon as 'the Jew' touches these things, the other mystical value comes to the fore and dispossesses him. Whilst the full range of social achievements and successes are potentially open to 'the Jew', in the face of the 'true' possessor, they not only count for nothing, but also reinforce their seeming valuelessness.

Again, the advantage for the antisemite is that, as 'organic' members of the nation, he can 'possess' and 'participate' in objects without the struggle or responsibility necessary to acquire them through rational means. The added value for the disenchanted member of the middle class is that, in his own imagination, he can merge with and become indistinguishable from the (real) ruling class, transforming what could never occur objectively.

> By treating the Jew as an inferior and pernicious being, I affirm at the same time that I belong to the elite. This elite, in contrast to those of modern times which are based on merit or labour, closely resemble an aristocracy of birth. There is nothing I have to do to merit my superiority, and neither can I lose it. It is given once and for all. It is a *thing*.
> (Sartre, 1995, p 27)

Not only modern forms of property ownership are revalued and devalued in this way. Other predicates of modernity, such as reason, intelligence, labour and merit, can be denigrated as 'Jewish', not only because they are deemed other to 'primitive' values, but also because they are associated with and came to dominate the social world at the same time as (and were the *means through which*) Jews were emancipated. From the perspective of the 'nation', of the antisemitic collective, these 'Jewish' values are always demeaned and, therefore, permit the antisemite to ignore them with impunity. The antisemite, now safely ensconced in the womb of community and having to their satisfaction escaped the fact and fate of responsibility, now come to associate fully modern society – its reason, its rationality, its equality, its rights, its property, its values and its difficulties – with 'the Jews'. The manner in which Sartre draws together these aspects of his argument is akin to

Nietzsche's portrait of the man of *ressentiment* and the system of evaluations he introduces into the world.

> But the way is open to me, mediocre me, to understand what the most subtle, the most cultivated intelligence has been unable to grasp. Why? Because I possess Racine – Racine and my country and my soil. Perhaps the Jew speaks a purer French than I do, perhaps he knows syntax and grammar better, perhaps he is even a writer. No matter, he has spoken this language for only twenty years. The correctness of his style is abstract, acquired. We recognize here the reasoning that Barres used against the holders of scholarship. Don't the Jews have all the scholarships? All that intelligence, all that money can acquire one leaves to them, but it is as empty as the wind. The only things that count are irrational values, and it is just these things which are denied the Jews forever. Thus, the anti-Semite takes his stand from the start on the ground of irrationalism. He is opposed to the Jew, just as sentiment is to intelligence, the particular to the universal, the past to the present, the concrete to the abstract, the owner of real property to the possessor of negotiable securities.
>
> (Sartre, 1995, p 25)

Yet, even from within the cocoon of the nation, the antisemite cannot relax; *ressentiment* continues to gnaw away at him. All notions of possession, even the irrationality of 'primitive possession', are never safe; there is always the risk of their being taken or stolen. From the perspective of the antisemite, the potential thief can only be the one who does not have 'true' or 'organic' title. The nation can never believe itself secure as long as the Jews and the values they bring with them continue to threaten the idyll; a threat that resides in the very impossibility of the Jew to escape his 'evil' essence. The 'real' country can never be declared safe and, in the form of offence, needs forever to be on the defensive against the sea of the 'legal' one.

Sartre remains sceptical, however, of the ability or willingness of the 'legal' country to offer support for those placed by the antisemite into the situation of 'the Jew'. Again, the concept of *ressentiment* is a central to Sartre's argument.

Drawing again on Marx's critique of the abstract nature of the Rights of Man and the Rights of the Citizen, Sartre argues that the Democrat – the figure who embodies the modern rule of law – is unable, or refuses, to recognise anyone other than in their abstract, autonomous form. Not only is the individual ripped from their *concrete* situation, but the very idea and presence of 'the Jew', antisemitism, or even a 'Jewish Question' remains unrecognised and, in effect, denied. In failing to offer the Jews legal and political recourse, this wilful blindness exacerbates the dangerous and difficult position in which they are placed.

It is in his prioritising of the abstract, universal concept of 'man', at the expense of any particularism that the Democrat exhibits his own *ressentiment* in the face of reality. So fearful is he of acknowledging the existence of conflict (be it social, that is, class conflict, or the idealism of antisemite and Jew) that, in refusing to act, he inverts the true relationship in accusing the Jew of undermining modern emancipation through demanding particularist treatment.

The Democrat's *ressentiment* when confronted with antisemitism surfaces particularly clearly in times of political and social crisis – the times, Sartre notes accurately, that coincide with an upsurge in antisemitism. At these moments, the Democrat affects a tolerant attitude to those who claim to speak in the name of, and for, 'national unity'. The very moment, therefore, that Jews are attacked *as Jews* and seek the protection of the 'legal country', they are turned away and sacrificed on the alter of 'unity' (Sartre, 1995, pp 55ff). It is at these moments that the nation usurps the emancipated body-politic, particularity negates universality, irrationality triumphs over rationality and myth over law; all of which are presided over by the Democrat. It is at this point that the emancipated Jew is caught between rights and *ressentiment*.

> The anti-Semite reproaches the Jew with *being Jewish*; the democrat reproaches him wilfully with *considering himself* a Jew. Between his enemy and his defender, the Jew is in a difficult situation: apparently, he can do not more than choose the sauce with which he will be devoured ... For a Jew, conscious and proud of being Jewish, asserting his claim to be a member of the Jewish community without ignoring on that account the bonds which unite him to the national community, there may not be much difference between the anti-Semite and the democrat. *The former wishes to destroy him as a man and leave nothing in him but the Jew, the pariah, the untouchable; the latter leave nothing in him but the man, the abstract and universal subject of the rights of man and the rights of the citizen.*
> (Sartre, 1995, pp 57–8; emphasis in original; emphasis added)

The question remains, as it did for Nietzsche, why it is around the figure of 'the Jew' that the discontents of a shortcoming of emancipation should crystallise? The answer Sartre provides turns on his argument, mentioned above, that the Jews 'entered history' through the means and transformations that brought about the modern, emancipated nation state. And so the *ressentiment* that arises from the shortcomings of political emancipation – the nature of *unemancipated* society as manifest in the domain of *private* property – attaches itself to 'the Jews'.

The *ressentiment* of the antisemite is evidenced further in Sartre's argument that the figure of the Jew is nothing more than the product of the antisemite's imagination, in which the Jew appears as a 'distortion' and as 'effigy'.

> In short, the essential thing here is not an 'historical fact', but the idea that the agents of history formed for themselves of the Jew ... It is, therefore, the *idea* of the Jew that one forms for himself which would seem to determine history, not the 'historical fact' that produces the idea.
> (Sartre, 1995, pp 15–16; emphasis in original)

It is at this point in the discussion that the equivocations noted at the beginning of this section appear in greater relief. The most obvious of these equivocations turns on Sartre's seeming agreement that the Jews cannot be treated as 'agents of history', a position reinforced by his acceptance of the idea that the Jews entered history in 1789 and their 'meaning' is defined solely in terms of their relationship to the antisemite. In fact, this view of the Jews has formed much of the criticism that has attached itself to *Anti-Semite and Jew*.[12] Rather than rehearsing that criticism, suffice it to say that Sartre's presentation of 'the Jews', like Nietzsche's, arises clearly from the perspective of the putative antisemite. The consequence is an account of antisemitism that, again like Nietzsche's, remains equivocal about the role and place of the Jews in moulding the world within which they live, no matter how hostile and no matter the ill intentions of other equally active social actors.

The core of this equivocation is the apparent acceptance of an ontology of loss that is endemic within emancipation and which, therefore, brings with it the possibility (and probability) of antisemitism. This equivocation is deepened rather than resolved in Sartre's call at the end of the work for a 'concrete liberalism' that, through the assimilation of all 'others', will result in an 'authentic community', or 'authentic nation'. It is as if Sartre's criticism of the antisemite is as much for constituting an *inauthentic* nation as it is for the hatred they direct to the Jews.

A further equivocation that exists between antisemitism and Sartre's account of it is the manner in which he *fixes* the categories of both 'anti-Semite' and 'Jew'. This setting in stone is reflected in Sartre's idea that to be included in one category or the other is the consequence of a choice that, once made, cannot be rescinded and becomes the very meaning or 'essence' of the individual. One becomes *either* a Jew *or* an anti-Semite *or* a Democrat. On this point, Sartre comes close to the antisemite's attempt to ontologise the products of the social world.[13]

It is in this context that Sartre brings to the fore a further characteristic that presents itself first in Nietzsche's connection between *ressentiment* and the

---

12 A good review of this criticism is in a special volume of the journal *October* (Winter 1999).
13 It is to be noted also that this ontologising of the categories appears to contradict the many empirical accounts of those who, in the aftermath of the Nazi takeover of power in Germany, could not believe so many of their previous friends and acquaintances should not only pass them on the street and join the party, but then, at the end of the war, resume contact as if nothing had happened (see Klemperer, 1999).

loss or denial of subjectivity; Nietzsche's concept of the 'herd' appears also in Sartre's account with its references to the antisemite's 'petrified values' and his desire to be like stone. As with Nietzsche, it is as if the claim of the antisemite to be a force of nature (albeit a nature petrified into a fixed and unchanging form), a force that cannot be stifled but only repressed, is left unchallenged. Again, one may wonder to what extent Sartre's own account of the pervasiveness (even if still only potential) of the ontological status of *antisemitism* itself incorporates a *ressentiment* against the condition of human nature that emancipation cannot alter.

These equivocations all appear in Sartre's conclusion to the section dedicated to 'the Anti-Semite' (and the correspondence both in sentiment and terminology to that of Nietzsche should not be overlooked).

> We are now in a position to understand the anti-Semite. He is a man who is afraid. Not of the Jews, to be sure, but of himself, of his own consciousness, of his liberty, of his instincts, of his responsibilities, of solitariness, of change, of society, of the world – of everything except the Jews. He is a coward who does not want to admit his cowardice to himself, a murderer who represses and censures his tendency to murder without being able to hold it back, yet who dares to kill only in effigy or protected by the anonymity of the mob; a malcontent who dares not revolt from fear of the consequences of his rebellion. In espousing anti-Semitism, he does not simply adopt an opinion, he chooses himself as a person. *He chooses the permanence and impenetrability of stone*, the total irresponsibility of the warrior who obeys his leaders – and he has no leader. He chooses to acquire nothing, to deserve nothing; he assumes that everything is given him as his birthright – and he is not noble. He chooses finally a Good that is fixed once and for all, beyond question and out of reach; he dares not examine it for fear of being led to challenge it and having to seek it in another form. The Jew only serves him as a pretext; elsewhere his counterpart will make use of the Negro or the man of yellow skin. The existence of the Jew merely permits the anti-Semite to stifle his anxieties at their inception by persuading himself that his place in the world has been marked out in advance, that it awaits him, and that tradition gives him the right to occupy it. Anti-Semitism, in short, is fear of the human condition. The anti-Semite is a man who wishes to be a pitiless stone, a furious torrent, a devastating thunderbolt – everything except a man.
> (Sartre, 1995, pp 53–4; emphasis added)

Lyotard: Auschwitz as ethics

Lyotard's contribution to critical accounts of antisemitism are contained in a series of books and articles written between the early 1980s and early 1990s. The immediate spur of his contemplation of antisemitism was a series of scandalous issues in France that grabbed popular and academic attention. The first of these episodes was the publication in 1981 of Faurisson's 'denial' of the existence of the gas chambers at Auschwitz. It was partly as an intervention in this controversy that Lyotard wrote and published *The Differend* in 1983. This dispute was followed a couple of years later by the so-called 'Heidegger Affair' which followed the publication of Victor Farias' indictment of the philosopher's commitment to National Socialism. It was as a contribution to this debate that Lyotard published *Heidegger and 'the jews'* in 1988. Finally, two articles published in 1990, *Europe, the Jews and the Book* and *The Grip* [*Mainisme*] comprise Lyotard's reflections on the desecration of the Jewish cemetery in Carpentras.

The cumulative effect of these controversies upon the realm of public affairs in France was great. They broke the silence around the Holocaust that had reigned for almost 40 years (since, in fact, Sartre's *Anti-Semite and Jew*). Along with the trial of Klaus Barbie, these 'affairs' challenged the orthodox self-representation of France as the nation of resistance and brought to light awkward questions of collaboration and responsibility. Lyotard's writing in response to these 'affairs' bears witness to the national trauma experienced there in the 1980s and 1990s.

Lyotard's thinking on antisemitism and the Holocaust turns on the idea that both phenomena are the product of a *ressentiment* deeply seated within the praxis of emancipation. In keeping with other thinkers in this tradition, Lyotard locates the origins of this product through the idea of loss or absence – in this instance, the loss or absence of 'the ethical'. However, what appears to distinguish Lyotard's account most is his belief that the targeting of this *ressentiment* against the Jews is not arbitrary, but is because the Jews are themselves the embodiment of this lost substance.

Several points emerge from Lyotard's work. First, if for Nietzsche antisemitism appears as a *potential* manifestation of *ressentiment* brought about by emancipation, and for Sartre it is the result of a *choice*, for Lyotard emancipation and antisemitism become far more integrated. A consequence of this merging is the substitution of a structural or 'objective' account of antisemitism for one that concentrates on the subject and subjectivity. Second, the deeper *ressentiment* and antisemitism are read into emancipation, the more *ressentiment* becomes a part of the critique itself. By this I mean that the sense of powerlessness and discomfort identified increasingly as the defining aspect of emancipation reappears in Lyotard's analysis. Third, and in consequence of and in proportion to these points, there is in Lyotard's work a reproduction of the antisemitic worldview. Again, this reproduction is seen in the ontologising of the loss Lyotard identifies in emancipation the idea of an ahistorical and asocial realm that exists beyond the 'artifice' of the body politic; and, finally, in the ontologising of 'the Jews' and 'Jewish values' that forever limits and obstructs their emancipation into wider society.

The irony of this last point is that the *ressentiment* that Lyotard unwittingly shares with antisemitism against emancipation gives rise correspondingly to a 'distorted' image or effigy of the Jews. The fact that Lyotard's work in general is philosemitic in character should not obscure this point. Lyotard gives to 'the Jews', antisemitism and the Holocaust the role Nietzsche gave to the slave: instigating an entirely new set of values. Interestingly, it is this ascribed role that leads to the paradoxical result (one prefigured in Nietzsche's reflections) of inaugurating an entirely new, post-Holocaust stream of anti-Jewish *ressentiment*.

Lyotard defines emancipation as the loss or absence of 'the ethical' – the obligation one has to the Other. Emancipation is the attempt to overcome this ontological heteronomy in the name of a humanist autonomy. It is in this sense of the term, therefore, that emancipation partakes of both the ontological and the historical, the site at which the two meet.

> The Christian Churches had introduced the motif of fraternity. The French Revolution extended it, by turning it on its head. We are brothers, not as sons of God but as free and equal citizens. It is not an Other who gives us the law. It is our civil community that does, that obliges, prohibits, permits. That is called emancipation for the Other, and autonomy. Our law opens citizenship to every individual, conditional on respect for republican virtues.
>
> (Lyotard, 1993d, pp 161–2)

As this list of modes of emancipation, of divesting 'Europe' from the obligation of a debt to the Other, indicates, the attempts are ultimately futile. Yet, it is precisely this futility that drives forward the endless search for peace, for having finally cancelled the debt.

Drawing on the language of psychoanalysis, Lyotard claims that rather than attaining such autonomy, emancipation acts to block or obstruct the ethical from coming into consciousness. This refusal does not, of course, negate the debt, but relocates it into the realm of the 'unconscious'. Its presence in the unconscious gives rise to a sense of unease, a feeling like a thorn in the flesh that Nietzsche describes as the 'bad conscience' and which matures into *ressentiment* and never ceases to be effective.

Lyotard offers the example of modern political emancipation with its discourse of rights, equality, rule of law and nation state which emerges from it.

> In speaking the law, [the legislator] decrees that he or she must respect it. In respecting the law, [the obligated one] decrees it anew. Their names, x and y, are in principle perfectly commutable between at least the two instances of normative addressor and prescriptive addressee. They are thus united in a single we ... The authorisation is then formulated thus:

> *We decree as a norm that it is an obligation for us to carry out act a.* This is the principle of autonomy.
>
> (Lyotard, 1988, p 98)

Yet, this attempt at emancipation and autonomy, as citizens becoming the masters of their own political fate, must fail because what is 'forgotten' (not only 'the ethical', but also the *loss* of the ethical itself), does not for the mere fact of being forgotten cease to exist. Buried and distributed within the realm of the unconscious, the forgotten makes itself felt in the realm of consciousness when, for no apparent reason, the latter feels assailed from the outside.

> The sudden feeling is as good as a testimony, through its unsettling strangeness, which 'from the exterior', lies in reserve in the interior, hidden away and from where it can on occasion depart to return from the outside to assail the mind as if it were issued not from it, but from the incidental situation.
>
> (Lyotard, 1988, pp 12–13)

In a manner of explanation that resembles the obsessions associated with a submerged, ontological origin and originating *ressentiment*, it is through this never-ending process that the autonomy which believes itself emancipated remains alert to the stirrings of its own unconscious connection with heteronomy, with the (irredeemable) debt to the Other. Because it cannot be ordered though consciousness, the (irrepressible) unconscious effect will appear as a 'bolt out of the blue'. Believing it has emancipated itself, consciousness will unexpectedly be seized by an anxiety which it cannot place. Yet this forgotten 'something', itself forgotten and buried in the unconscious, is continually present as a lack, or *lapsus*, within consciousness. And, in turn, consciousness will continually respond to an unconscious desire to be rid of that which its senses, but does not know and which disrupts its search for autonomy. By associating antisemitism and the Holocaust with this obsessional *ressentiment* brought about by the unacknowledged persistent irritation of the forgotten loss of the ethical, Lyotard places these events *beyond* and in *excess* of 'the political'.

> The solution was to be final: the final answer to the 'Jewish' question. It was necessary to carry it right up to its conclusion, to 'terminate' the interminable. And thus to 'terminate' the term itself. It had to be the perfect crime, one would plead not guilty, certain for the lack of proofs. This is a 'politics' of absolute forgetting, forgotten. Absurd, since its very zeal, its very desperation distinguishes it as extra-political. Obviously, a politics of extermination exceeds politics. It is not negotiated on a scene. This obstinacy to exterminate to the very end, because it cannot be

understood politically, already indicates that we are dealing with something else, with the Other.

(Lyotard, 1990, p 25)

It is to be noted that in the context of the paragraph as a whole, the figure of 'the Other' appears to contain several distinct meanings, all of which throw light on Lyotard's presentation of antisemitism and the Holocaust. The most obvious meaning, of course, is 'the Other' as the Jews. A second meaning of 'the Other' is as the ethical, that which is denied and absented by emancipation; and, finally, 'the Other' points to the excluded or denied 'one' to whom the debt is owed. All these three meanings combine to form Lyotard's conception of 'the Jews'.

In presenting the Jews through this triad of associations, Lyotard focuses on the Jews' founding moment as 'the Jews'. He argues that this founding took place through:

> a promise and an alliance that are not the contract and the pact, a promise made to a people who did not want it and had no need of it, an alliance that has not been negotiated, that goes against the people's interests, of which it knows itself unworthy. And do this people, an old communal apparatus, already well-to-do, hypothetically, with intact defence mechanisms and dynamic, economic, linguistic regulations without which it would not be a people, this simple people taken hostage by a voice that does not tell it anything, save it (this voice) is, and that all representation and naming of it are forbidden, and that it, the people, only needs listen to its tone, to be obedient to a timbre.
>
> (Lyotard, 1988, p 21)

It is worth at this moment, comparing Lyotard's depiction of the Jews' founding with a succinct and accurate account of Lyotard's concept of the ethical in which any sense of 'dialectic' is ruled out of court. Lyotard translates ethical obligations as a phrase that puts its addressee in the position of being obliged, that is, of being solely the addressee of the phrase and the addressor of a reaction to the phrase. In obligation, the addressee is solely a 'you' as in the phrase, 'You must obey'; there is no corresponding phrase of the form 'I must obey', where the self becomes a subject again prior to obeying.

The final meaning of 'the Other' and its association with 'the Jews' is the idea that the originating 'Call' was so traumatic that it could not be registered within consciousness. Forbidden to be represented, the Other (the Voice) remains beyond and unknown to consciousness. Never able to be recognised or named, it lingers as a feeling that exceeds all knowledge and all language. The purpose of the Jews' 'Book' (in which this origin is recounted) is, therefore, *not* to represent (to recognise and name) the Other, through which the debt and obligation to the Other would be cancelled, but rather is constantly to remind the Jews that they have 'forgotten the Forgotten'. As a consequence, the Jews are eternally reminded of their debt to the Other, if only in the sense of being reminded that they have forgotten that debt.

The Jews, therefore, distinct from all other European peoples, come to bear the multilayered role of 'the Other', which makes them the foil of any attempt at emancipation and autonomy (including their own), and imposes upon them the function of lightning conductor for unaccountable and unpredictable flashes of *ressentiment*.

> Thus it is that the Jews cannot manage to find their place in the systems by which thought is represented in the politics and social practices of the European West. They cannot form a 'nation' in the medieval sense, nor a people in the modern sense. The Law forbids them to acquire the communitarian status of an ethnic group. The relation of the Event of the Covenant and the Promise is a relation of dependence, not a relation to a land and a history, but a relation to the letters of a book and to a paradoxical temporality.
>
> (Lyotard, 1993c, p 143)

From this perspective, therefore, the Jews appear to exist 'within' Europe in the same manner as the ethical is said to exist in its connection with consciousness. They exist as the 'absent-present' that exceeds politics but which, nonetheless, is deeply entrenched within the unconscious of Europe. As such, their 'presence' appears within Europe's unconscious as an undefined and indefinable challenge, forever limiting and calling into question its self-proclaimed autonomy. The *ressentiment* that rains down upon the Jews and which increases in proportion to the depth of emancipation claimed is, in the final analysis, intimately connected to the role of the Jews, less as the conscience of Europe, but more its 'bad conscience'. It is a role, moreover, that is itself a product of their very constitution and continued existence as Jews. Antisemitism and emancipation are two sides of the same coin.

> Anti-Semitism is one of the means of the apparatus of its culture to bind and represent as much as possible – to protect against – the originary terror, actively to forget it. It is the defensive side of its attack mechanisms – Greek science, Roman law and politics, Christian spirituality, and the Enlightenment, the underside of knowledge, of having, of wanting, of hope. One converts the Jews in the Middle Ages, they resist by mental restriction. One expels them during the classical age, they return. One integrates them in the modern era, they persist in their difference. One exterminates them in the twentieth century.
>
> (Lyotard, 1993c, p 23)

It is after locating the ethical, the Jews, antisemitism and the Holocaust within the realm of the unconscious that the third meaning of 'the Other' comes to the fore. 'The Other' is the one to whom the debt is owed.

Lyotard is insistent that the impossibility of representing 'Auschwitz' does not mean that this 'event' is forgotten. Auschwitz leaves its trace as a 'feeling', as something so traumatic, so sudden, so absolute and so total that it remains beyond 'genres of discourse' – in other words, beyond consciousness. Lyotard explains that the word 'Auschwitz' must be treated as a 'sign', a sign of 'something' which cannot be grasped or understood. It becomes a 'sign' that throws into doubt any notion of 'autonomy', any sense that this 'event' could be assimilated into and mastered by and through consciousness.

> Signs are not referents to which are attached significations validatable under the cognitive regimen, they indicate that something which should be able to be put into phrases cannot be phrased in the accepted idioms. That, in a phrase universe, the referent be situated as a sign that has as a corollary that in the same universe the addressee is situated like someone who is affected, and that the sense is situated like an unresolved problem, an enigma perhaps, a mystery or a paradox – this feeling does not arise from an experience felt by a subject.
>
> (Lyotard, 1988, p 57)

In presenting the Holocaust in this way, Lyotard is making of it something akin to the initial Call that he sees as founding 'the Jews'. Both are beyond the realm of consciousness, of thought, of knowledge and of politics. Both the Holocaust and the Jews become the Forgotten that cannot be forgotten, that which is not dissolved but which remains within the unconscious. It is for this reason that Lyotard's own writing on this subject is not to record 'what happened', but rather is to record the fact that we must remember that we have forgotten the forgotten, the existence of the debt as well as the one to whom the debt is owed. Lyotard's own writings, therefore, are modelled on those of the Jewish 'book'.

In all these ways, antisemitism and the Holocaust, like the Jews, become effective in terms of 'the ethical'; they become the trauma, the inassimilable and unrepresentable Call to heteronomy that all attempts at autonomy cannot erase. It is a trauma that Lyotard believes can be traced back to a praxis of emancipation that contains within its very meaning, the loss of the ethical. It is this loss that, pushed into the recesses of the unconscious, matures into a *ressentiment* that, unknown and unknowingly, erupts with such terrible vengeance and consequences upon the memory of that loss – the Jews.

I noted in the introduction to this chapter that the more emancipation is marred with *ressentiment*, the more the critique itself exhibits the same tendency.

Lyotard's replication of *ressentiment* appears most overtly in his belief in an ontological and irreparable fault lying within the very essence of emancipation that gives rise to the *ressentiment* of antisemitism. In accepting the existence of the loss that he identifies – the loss of the ethical – as well as its inability to be recouped within an emancipated world, Lyotard is exhibiting the same sense of powerlessness, of negative acceptance, and which leads to a pessimism if not paralysis of action that are the hallmarks not only of *ressentiment* in general but of the *ressentiment* of antisemitism in particular. I have commented on the presence of *ressentiment* in Nietzsche and Sartre, most notably upon their replication of antisemitic assumptions (but not values), and it is interesting to see that the depth of replication is directly proportionate to the depth of *ressentiment* exhibited by each in his initial critique of emancipation.

In Lyotard's case, first and foremost is the idea that not only must emancipation fail, but it can only bring *ressentiment* and antisemitism (not to say genocide) in its wake. It is often in these terms that, although diametrically opposed to Lyotard's intentions, the antisemite warns the Jews primarily against any attempt to change the status quo. Further, Lyotard presents unintentionally the antisemitic picture of the Jews as inherently unassimilable into a society premised and organised around universalist, abstract and formal principles, such as rights and the rule of law. There is 'something about' the Jews, in other words, something existing at the level of ontology that makes them incapable of partaking in such a society.

> What then can a 'French or German citizen of Israelite profession' be – above all if he is an officer like Dreyfus or a head of government like Blum? In the European unconscious, it is recognised that his debt to the Other will prevail over his duties to the others, to the national community. And that he is bound to be a potential traitor. Unless he forgets himself as a Jew. This is the great temptation for the 'assimilated' themselves. The 'final solution' will come as a monstrous reminder to them that they are always *even despite themselves*, witnesses to something about which Europe wants to know nothing.
> (Lyotard, 1993d, p 161; emphasis added)

Lyotard's portrait of the Jews is as much a 'distortion' or 'effigy' as that painted by antisemites. The idea of 'the Jews' as the embodiment – if not of the ethical itself, then at the least the trace of the ethical – is as artificial as the image of the Jews as the incarnation of evil. Lyotard's 'positive' image is as much a product of *ressentiment* as the antisemite's image. What distinguishes Lyotard from the antisemitic man of *ressentiment*, however, is not his understanding of emancipation, nor his attribution of specific Jewish 'characteristics', but is rather their *valuation*. Both the antisemite and Lyotard divide the world between 'good' and 'evil', but the difference between them lies in the fact that for Lyotard it is 'the Jews' who are the embodiment of 'good'. Yet, as the following discussion will illustrate, the *effect* of the image – 'good' or 'evil' – remains frighteningly similar in its outcomes.

Perhaps the most disturbing element of the elevation of the Holocaust and the Jews to the status of 'the ethical', of a debt that can never be paid and which remains buried within the unconscious as a 'feeling', is the intrusion of a *ressentiment* against the Jews in critical discussions of the Holocaust.

As already discussed, Lyotard's meaning of the Holocaust is at one with his depiction of the initial Call that constituted Jews as *the* Jews. Both are said to remain beyond or in excess of consciousness, thought, knowledge or politics; in short, beyond representation. In relation to the Holocaust, therefore, Lyotard's writing serves the same purpose as he sees in the praxis of the 'Jewish book'. His writing of the Holocaust is aimed not to write of history (no matter how broadly defined), but to make us, the reader, remember that we have forgotten this forgotten (Auschwitz), to remind us that we are 'always already' in debt to an Other, and, moreover, that the debt can never be paid and the Other never recognised. The sense of unpaid debt the Jews owed to their own 'Addressor' who constituted them as 'the Jews' is, following their destruction, now transferred to the 'sign' of 'Auschwitz' and to its role in constituting the already existing people of Europe into 'the Europeans', who will never forget their debt to the Other – not the Jews, but 'Auschwitz', it is a debt to themselves, to their own 'bad conscience'.

What is most striking about Lyotard's account is not so much his implication that, following the Holocaust, the debt to the Jews has been settled (itself a possible expression of Lyotard's own unconscious desire to cancel the debt to the Other), but that, in leaving the nature or essence of the ethical in place, he did not anticipate a corresponding presence of *ressentiment* against antisemitism and the Holocaust. The paradox at the heart of Lyotard's thesis is his belief that, through the extermination of the Jews at the middle of the twentieth century, Europe has *finally and irrevocably* been emancipated from them. It is this belief that lies at the heart of his idea that Auschwitz and Europe have been exchanged for the God of the Old Testament and the Jews respectively. It is as a consequence of this exchange that, at a time in which 'we' are all indebted to Auschwitz, to a debt that can never be repaid, those whose presence is a reminder that this 'we' have, in fact, forgotten the forgotten (and this includes not just 'Auschwitz' but those for whom Auschwitz was brought into being – the Jews) will, since again it is located within 'Europe's unconscious', be met by *ressentiment*. As before, the 'we' (that is, 'Europe') will vent its frustration with the failure of yet another attempt to be emancipated from the ethical and of remaining in debt. Frustration will rise, in other words, of not being rid of 'the Jews'. It is this *ressentiment* not against the Holocaust itself (that is, Holocaust *denial*), but against the fact of its Jewish specificity that is embodied in the term 'Holocaust dissolution'.

Holocaust dissolution points to the *ressentiment* that arises at the limits of this latest attempt at emancipation from the Jews through a denial of the specificity of Jewish suffering as well as its cause, the reality of antisemitism. In so doing, it erases from accounts of the Holocaust those who not only died as Jews (including those who did not consent to such labelling), but also to the entire history of modern antisemitism and its connection to modern political, social and cultural conditions. Like the ideal of antisemitism itself, therefore, Holocaust dissolution denies the entire existence of Jews in the modern world, not in the Sartrean sense of antisemitism producing 'the Jew', but in the Arendtian sense of Jews as active agents in the continuing making of the world (including that of a world in which antisemitism is present). Finally, the denial of Jewish specificity serves to disarm claims of the existence of the actuality and potentiality of contemporary antisemitism, even when, or especially when, those claims turn on the argument that their protagonists have forgotten the forgotten of the Holocaust.

Giorgio Agamben: from Holocaust to Auschwitz to the *Musselman*

The notion of Holocaust dissolution, of *ressentiment* against a specifically Jewish dimension to the Nazi mass exterminations, appears most clearly in Giorgio Agamben's *Remnants of Auschwitz: the Witness and the Archive*. It is in that work that the extermination of the Jews (and not only the Jews) is dislodged as the central aim and purpose of Nazism, and is replaced in its stead by the figure of the *Musselman* as the key to understanding the enigma of 'Auschwitz'.

In the discussion that follows, it is important to bear in mind that the *ressentiment* Agamben's work exhibits to the Holocaust (or the *Shoah*) is not the product or consequence of a *ressentiment* against the Jews, past, present or future. It is, rather, the outcome of a *ressentiment* that lies deep within his own theoretical perspective; a *ressentiment* that he identifies as the hidden core and driving force of modern emancipation.

Following in the footsteps of Nietzsche, Sartre and Lyotard, Agamben's depiction of emancipation turns on the idea of an originating loss containing an ensuing *ressentiment*. For Agamben, the loss is of nature or, more accurately, of the 'mysteries' of nature, particularly the mysteries associated with natality.

This sense of loss, and the *ressentiment* that accompanies it, is premised upon two intimately connected components of what Agamben means by 'emancipation'. The first meaning is that of an autonomous nature associated with the mysteries of birth. The second, and almost as the precondition for such mystery, is the location of natality within the realm of the private (in this instance, the household). It is, in other words, this *double* meaning of emancipation – emancipation from nature and emancipation from the private sphere of the home – that is, for Agamben, the key to understanding the modern emancipated world.

With the advent of modernity, nature and natality were to become the concern, definition and meaning of the political concept of sovereignty. It is this coming together of life and politics that Agamben sees as the essence of 'biopolitics',[14] a form of governance he sees as without precedent.

> The same bare life that in the *ancien regime* was politically neutral and belonged to God as creaturely life and in the classical world was (at least apparently) clearly distinguished as *zoe* from political life (*bios*) now fully enters into the structure of the state and even becomes the earthly foundation of the state's legitimacy and sovereignty.
>
> (Agamben, 1998, p 127)

Agamben offers in this context the following interpretation of the significance and meaning of the Rights of Man and the Rights of the Citizen.

> Declarations of rights represent the originary figure of the inscription of natural life in the juridico-political order of the nation-state ... the fiction here is that *birth* immediately becomes *nation*, such that there can be no interval or separation [*scarto*] between the two terms. Rights are attributed to man (or originate in him) solely to the extent that man is the immediately vanishing ground (who must never come to light as such) of the citizen.
>
> (Agamben, 1998, pp 127–8)

It was through the prism of biopolitics that the question of who was to be included within the nation state and who was to be excluded was decided.

Although Agamben does not present his argument in these terms, it is clear that developments in biopolitics were becoming increasingly driven by a *ressentiment* against the merest presence or hint of an autonomous nature, of a 'free' realm of birth, seeping into the seemingly hermeneutically sealed realm of 'the political'. More and more, the *political* question which Agamben treats as the Schmittian question of sovereignty – he who decides on the exception – came to be colonised by the dictates and practices of the biological sciences. Understood from this perspective, the determining racism of the Third Reich – with its concurrent radicalising of the boundary between inclusion and exclusion, a radicalism that translated literally into the question of life and death respectively – is cut loose from any specific historical causality and, instead, is presented as a 'paradigm' case of the nature of modern emancipation itself. It is an emancipation whose obsessive *ressentiment* against birth has brought with it the proliferation of death.

---

14 See above, Chapter 2.

I have already discussed elsewhere[15] the loss of specificity brought about by the treatment of the Holocaust as a paradigm. However, an even further move towards such a loss of a specifically *Jewish* aspect and Jewish *engagement* with these events is introduced in Agamben's *Remnants of Auschwitz*. Here the true horror and unprecedented nature of Nazism is not, or not only, the production of dead bodies, the majority of whom were murdered as Jews, but the production of an entirely new, that is, *modern*, form of life – the *Musselman*.

> It is then possible to understand the *decisive function* of the camps and the system of *Nazi biopolitics*. They are not merely [*sic*] the place of death and extermination; they are also, *and above all*, the site of the production of the *Musselman*, the *final* biopolitical substance to be isolated in the biological continuum. Beyond the *Musselman* lies only the gas chamber.
> (Agamben, 2002, p 85; emphasis added)

It is in the creation of the *Musselman* that the previous division between 'Jew' and 'Aryan', of exclusion and inclusion, that Agamben saw as the paradigm of biopolitics in general, is no longer presented as an 'end in itself' but, rather, as a 'means to a further end'. The murder of the Jews loses meaning in itself and becomes 'merely' a step along the way to something even more 'momentous', the birth of an entirely new form of life.

> Biopolitical caesuras are essentially mobile, and in each case they isolate a further zone in the biological continuum, a zone which corresponds to a process of increasing *Erdwurdigung* and degradation. Thus, the non-Aryan passes into the Jew, the Jew into the deportee (*ungeisedelt, ausgesiedelt*), the deportee into the prisoner (*Hatfling*), until biopolitical caesuras reach their final limit in the camp. *This limit is the* Musselman. At the point at which the *Hatfling* becomes a *Musselman*, the biopolitics of racism so to speak transcends race, penetrating into a threshold in which it is no longer possible to establish caesuras, and *we witness the emergence of something like an absolute biological substance that cannot be assigned to a particular bearer or subject, or divided by another caesura*.
> (Agamben, 2002, pp 84–5; non-German emphasis added)

With the figure of the *Musselman*, Agamben appears to be cancelling any and all debts previously connected with a specifically Jewish dimension to Nazism, antisemitism and the Holocaust. Lyotard's claim that with Nazism 'Europe' has finally emancipated itself from the Jews receives its theoretical expression thus:

---

15 See above, Chapter 2.

> Listening to something absent did not provide fruitless work for this author. Above all, it made it necessary to clear away almost all the doctrines that, since Auschwitz, have been advanced in the name of ethics ... almost none of the ethical principles of our age believed it could recognise as valid stood the *decisive* step, that of an *Ethica more Auschwitz demonstrata*.
>
> (Agamben, 2002, p 13)

As a consequence of this interpretation of 'Auschwitz', Agamben comes closest to replicating the central aim and purpose of antisemitism: to erase any trace of 'the Jews'' existence in the world. This replication of antisemitic praxis presents itself not only in their disappearance *as Jews* from within the world of the camps themselves (can they any longer be called *extermination camps?*),[16] but it also erases all their traces from the history of modern emancipation and the body politics that developed in its wake and with their imprint.

Paradoxically, what lies at the core of Agamben's *ressentiment* against the recognition or acknowledgement of a specifically Jewish dimension to the Holocaust is the same as that which he believes he has unearthed at the core of modern emancipation. This *ressentiment* turns upon the almost obsessive striving to emancipate humanity from the 'mysteries of birth' and the private realm in which it remains shrouded. As the sole and unique product of the essence of this emancipation – biopolitics – only the *Musselman* meets these criteria.

At this point, one can detect the causes for Agamben's own *ressentiment*. Despite his attempts in both *Homo Sacer* and *State of Exception* to present the Jews as brought into being (if only at the same moment as their deaths) through the immediacy of biopolitics, the possibility of their prior or external existence can never be entirely discounted. Just as the possibility of such contamination is said to drive the *ressentiment* at the heart of biopolitics, that is, at the heart of modern emancipation, so too can it be seen at play in Agamben's own work.

This potential 'breaching of the walls' of both emancipation and the critique of emancipation is apparent throughout the entire edifice Agamben constructs around the praxis of biopolitics. Located in a series of 'thresholds' (from the Sovereign State of Exception through the camp to the *Musselman* itself) that is defined by its existence in a nether world of indistinction, this praxis can only be grasped ontologically as if biopolitics had really succeeded in its emancipation from nature and from the private realm. It is with the introduction of the Jews into this isolated landscape that such 'success' is

---

16 For a discussion of the generic use of 'camp' in Agamben's work, see Mesnard, 2004, pp 139–57.

brought into question. Despite all arguments to the contrary and despite the draining of all particularity that their status as a 'paradigm' implies, the specificity of real Jews (as against that of their ontological, 'biopolitical' existence) must remain (both literally and theoretically).

For both Agamben and the nature of emancipation he presents, to recognise or acknowledge a modern Jewish specificity – socially, politically, and culturally, both independent of and connected with antisemitism and the Holocaust – would mean recognising or acknowledging the limits of both emancipation and critique. It is as a consequence of these processes that the *ressentiment* of the one transfers itself into the *ressentiment* of the other. It is this, perhaps, that underpins Agamben's philologically informed self-prohibition 'why we will never make use of the term [the Holocaust],[17] and, in so doing, rob the language of one of the most recognisable signifiers for the crimes against the Jews committed by the Nazis across the width and breadth of continental Europe.

It is this coincidence of *ressentiment* that comes together in Agamben's account of the *Musselman*. It is as if the *ressentiment* against nature that Agamben sees as the driving force of modern emancipation has produced a being in its own image. Taken as a whole, Agamben's depictions of the *Musselman* is nothing other than a reflection of a power of creation that, for all its efforts, for all its work, has yet to uncover the true mysteries of birth, the 'divine spark' that makes one human. Born of *ressentiment* it carries the mark of its progenitor in its body.

It is as if the creation of the *Musselman* is the hubristic embodiment of emancipation's driven *ressentiment* against nature's claim to be the sole creator, not only of life, but of *new forms of life*. For Agamben, the novelty of the *Musselman* is his existing in the realm 'between' or 'beyond' life and death. It is, moreover, a creation like 'man' [Adam] who himself, according to Biblical texts, is a creation made in the image of his Maker, a figure of total domination; the domination of nature.

In terms that recall Nietzsche's definition of the man of *ressentiment*, the *Musselman* is the mute witness of a powerlessness that, in the face of absolute power, remains. And finally on this point, it is this absolute slave-like nature of the *Musselman* from which Agamben wishes to simultaneously devalue the entire range of existing ethics and to inaugurate an entirely new code or 'new ethics'.

The paradox of Agamben's approach and conclusion is that the full and final moment of exchange that he seeks between the modern world and the world to come and which he sees as turning on the figure of the *Musselman*, is premised upon, and leaves untouched, a sense of an original and originating ontological loss. Far from settling the debts of the past, the question of the

---

17 Cf Nietzsche, 2002, I:5.

specifically Jewish dimension to the Holocaust remains the ensuing original loss, buried deep within and hidden behind the new universalism of the *Musselman* of the State of Exception and of the camp and in whose name a new ethical world is inaugurated. The slave again stands in the place of the noble.

As a consequence of this loss, there emerges a new bad conscience and a new *ressentiment*. In this instance, the drive of this *ressentiment* is the rooting out and obsessive denial of the Holocaust as marking a specifically Jewish connection to the Nazi mass exterminations. The irony of this *ressentiment* is that, just as Agamben and, to a lesser extent, Lyotard have sought an ethics that is dependent upon the emancipation of 'Auschwitz' from its Jewish aspects, so will the 'new' ressentiment re-establish such links. Behind the universality of the *Musselman* there will always be suspected the presence of the Jew. It was Bruno Bauer who, over a century and a half ago and decades before the term 'antisemitic' was uttered, offered a glimpse of what can follow from an emancipation that does not recognise its own limits and its own equivocalities.

> 'Very well,' it is said, and the Jew himself says it, 'the Jew is to become emancipated not as a Jew, not because he is a Jew, not because he possesses such an excellent, universally human principle of morality; on the contrary, the *Jew* will retreat behind the *citizen* and be a *citizen*, although he is a Jew and is to remain a Jew. That is to say, he is and remains a *Jew*, although he is a *citizen* and lives in universally human conditions: his Jewish and restricted nature triumphs always in the end over his human and political obligations. The *prejudice* remains in spite of being outstripped by *general* principles. But if it remains, then, on the contrary, it outstrips everything else.'
>
> 'Only sophistically, only apparently, would the Jew be able to remain a Jew in the life of the state. Hence, if he wanted to remain a Jew, the mere appearance would become the essential and would triumph; that is to say, his *life in the state* would be only a semblance or only a temporary exception to the essential and the rule.'
>
> (quoted in Marx, 1992, p 214)

Conclusion

What comes to light most clearly in this essay is the presentation of antisemitism as the outcome of a shortcoming of emancipation that, in itself, has little or nothing to do with the actual existence of Jews. In these reworkings of the 'scapegoat' thesis,[18] the Jews become the target for a *ressentiment* that

---

18 See above, Chapter 2.

has its origins within a perceived loss or absence within the core of emancipation. The limits of emancipation thus account for the correspondence of the image of the Jews present in both the antisemitic imagination and its critique.

It is interesting to note also the lessening of the gap or distance between emancipation and antisemitism. This point becomes clear through consideration of the means of mediation that is said to connect the two. For Nietzsche, emancipation and antisemitism are related through a series of exchanges, whilst for Sartre the connection is the product of a single and seemingly irretrievable 'choice'. It is after the Holocaust,[19] however, that this tendency to bring the two together is radicalised. For Lyotard, therefore, antisemitism, as *ressentiment* against the loss of 'the ethical', exists and is buried deep within the nature of emancipation itself, whilst for Agamben emancipation and antisemitism are seamlessly folded one into the other.

The consequence of Agamben's position is that the *ressentiment* expressed against emancipation by both antisemitism and the critic of antisemitism engulfs antisemitism and the Holocaust. Subsumed under universal categories, the specificity of antisemitism and the Holocaust will become the ontological loss that lies at the core of the calls for an emancipation from emancipation. The consequence of this new loss contains within it *ressentiment* against the acknowledgement of a specifically modern Jewish dimension to the equivocalities of emancipation. It is a *ressentiment* that we find nurtured within the very roots of antisemitism itself.

---

19 Whilst it is true that Sartre's work was written during the liberation of France, it is the case also that he appears not to have fully comprehended the sheer scale of the atrocities that comprise the Holocaust (see Tenzo, 1999).

Chapter 5

The slave, the noble and the Jew: reflections on section 7 of *On the Genealogy of Morals*

Introduction

The ambit of this chapter is clearly circumscribed; it is a re-appraisal and re-evaluation of the allegations of anti-Judaism or antisemitism in section 7 of the first essay of *On the Genealogy of Morals*,[1] 'Good and Bad', 'Good and Evil'. It is in this section that the Jews, there characterised as 'that priestly people', are given the role of overcoming the noble in the name of the slave and replacing the former's mode of evaluation of 'good and bad' with that of 'good and evil'.

The reasons for this seemingly narrow focus are twofold. First, as have many others, I have always been puzzled not just by the anti-Judaic and antisemitic sentiments Nietzsche expresses in that section, but also the venom with which they are expressed. My sense of puzzlement only increases when section 7 is set aside Nietzsche's oft-expressed and evidently sincere opposition to contemporaneous antisemitism.[2] The enigmatic nature of this seeming contradiction is brought into even greater relief when set against the fact that Nietzsche was amongst the first commentators to identify, chronicle and offer a diagnosis of this phenomenon.

The second reason for my choice of focus stems from my dissatisfaction with the manner in which the proliferating commentaries on Nietzsche's work treat this issue. On the one hand, many of them simply choose to bypass the very real problems that section 7 raises.[3] More often than not, they are dealt with perfunctorily through noting Nietzsche's philosemitic or anti-antisemitic credentials.[4] On the other hand, there are those accounts that address the issue directly but in isolation from other aspects of his thought. The general consensus of this strand of thinking is to emphasise Nietzsche's

---

1 Nietzsche, 2002.
2 For examples and illustrations, see Yovel, 1994 and 1998. For an extended debate on this question and related issues, see also Golomb, 1997 and Golomb and Wistrich, 2002.
3 See Conway, 1997 and Leiter, 2002.
4 See, inter alia, Safranski, 2002; Wicks, 2002; Ansell-Pearson, 1994.

'ambivalent' attitude toward the Jews.[5] This conclusion is premised upon the idea that Nietzsche distinguishes and evaluates three different periods within the internal history of 'the Jews': the biblical, the priestly and the modern. Sympathetic and complimentary to the first and last, section 7 represents his distaste of the middle period. Even if this were the case, and one of the aims of this essay is to open this account to question, it still does not fully account for the hostility manifested by Nietzsche.

In contradistinction to both these approaches, this essay argues that section 7 has *nothing whatsoever to say about the Jews*. However, it does contain a great deal of insight about the antisemite. This argument is premised upon reading this work in the spirit in which it was written, that is, *genealogically* and *polemically*. Treating genealogy[6] as the ability to unmask[7] the diverse types whose will to power constitutes the meaning of words, concepts and ideas, a link is established between the fate of the concept 'good' and the fate of the figure of the 'noble'. In both instances, Nietzsche's genealogy illustrates that the meaning of these concepts are expressions of the same type, the slave or man of *ressentiment*.

Nietzsche's self-styled description of the *Genealogy* as a polemic draws on two of the word's common meanings. The first, a controversial and disputatious contribution to an ongoing theological debate, is evidenced by his insistence of the non-divine origins of morality.

The second meaning of 'polemic' which applies to the *Genealogy* (and to Nietzsche's writings as a whole) is its style of almost warlike confrontation with the objects of critique: the Church, Richard Wagner, Eugen Duhring, moralists, cultural philistines, and so on. One of the weapons utilised to great effect by Nietzsche in these wars was that of irony,[8] as the case of the noble indicates. Gillian Rose's description of Adorno's *Minima Moralia* is an example of how irony is useful as polemic:

> [it] is ironic in the two standard senses of the word: 'expression of meaning by use of words normally conveying the opposite meaning', and 'apparent perversity of fate or circumstance' ... Sometimes he uses

---

5 Yovel, 1994 and 1998; Duffy and Mittleman, 1988. It is interesting to note that this evaluative typology is also found in Deleuze, 1983 which, in almost all other ways, offers an iconoclastic view of such historical accounts. For criticisms of this tripartite approach, see Brinker, 2002 and Rose, 1993, 'Nietzsche's *Judaica*'.
6 Whilst discussions and interpretations of the meaning of Nietzsche's genealogy appear in almost all commentaries of his work, useful collections of essays include Schact, 1994 and Richardson, 2001 (a collection that includes Michel Foucault's 'Nietzsche, genealogy, history').
7 For a discussion of the importance of masks to understanding Nietzsche, see Williams, 1978. See also MacIntyre in Schact 1994.
8 For a fuller discussion of Nietzsche's use of irony, see Rose, 1978.

the original phrase and conveys the ironic inversion in the discussion. Sometimes he just states the inversion and does not discuss it.

(Rose, 1978, p 26)

Reading section 7 ironically, the tactic of ironic inversion becomes increasingly visible: what appears as the voice of the noble is unmasked as that of the slave, as the man of *ressentiment*. This irony of misrecognition is doubled when the reader realises that, as a man of *ressentiment*, the noble is unable to see himself as such. On this realisation, a further irony presents itself. Far from the noble's self-representation offering a challenge to the decadence of contemporary culture, Nietzsche shows how this noble is, rather, an expression of its exhaustion.

This genealogy of the noble is constituted through a comparison of two of Nietzsche's most sustained commentaries on this figure, both of which are centred around the person and persona of Richard Wagner: *The Birth of Tragedy* and the first essay of *On the Genealogy of Morals*. The first section of this current work offers a depiction of the noble in the earlier study. The second compares and contrasts this descriptive and normative account with that provided in the *Genealogy*. The essay concludes with a discussion of the impact this genealogy has for recognising Nietzsche as one of the earliest analysts and critics of the modern phenomenon of antisemitism.

The genealogy of the noble: *The Birth of Tragedy*

Nietzsche's earliest sustained treatment of the noble is found in his study *The Birth of Tragedy*. It may be noted as others have, however, that it could be better titled 'the *Re*-birth of Tragedy'. Having traced its birth and demise in the context of ancient Greece, Nietzsche sees the possibility of the potential revival of tragedy in the Germany of the time under the auspices of whom he believed to be the new tragic noble, Richard Wagner.

Nietzsche located the expression of the glories of pre-Socratic Greek in the mythologies articulated through the art of their great tragedies. These mythologies reflected the strength of the Ancient Greeks and their culture built upon the edifice of a terrible and potentially overawing power of a raw and directionless nature. The greatness of the tragedies lay in drawing all involved, actors and spectators, into the immediacy of these creative-destructive forces. Expressing this phenomenon through the gods Dionysus and Apollo, Nietzsche argued that:

> [t]he Dionysiac is the basic ground of the world and the foundation of all existence. In the final analysis, it must be thought of as the eternal and original artistic power that calls into being the entire world of phenomena. The Apolline is secondary, the source of those illusions with which the Dionysiac world must, for our own sakes, be transfigured. As far as

human awareness is concerned, the two impulses manifest themselves in a strict relation: only so much Dionysiac experience is permitted to the individual consciousness as can be controlled by the Apolline and translated into self-sustaining terms. The present emergence of the Dionysiac thus implies the co-presence of the Apolline and, in turn, an efflorescence of Apolline art in the years ahead. The scale and perfection of the Apolline manifestations among the Greeks, conversely, attests the powerful hold that the Dionysiac must have among them. Let us bear in mind how much they must have suffered to achieve such beauty. Above all, let us acknowledge the two principles, Dionysiac and Apolline, as the basis of tragedy, their highest achievement.

(Silk and Stern, 1981, p 88)

This 'golden age' was brought low through the historical intervention of the figure of Socrates. The effect of Socratic reason and rationality was to block life from the danger and spontaneity of Dionysian nature. Nature, human and otherwise, now became an object of enquiry through which its apparent purpose could be divined and chance substituted by order. The death of the old tragedy of pathos was replaced by the new tragedy of logos (Safranski, 2002, p 63), the Dionysian laid low by the Apolline, and myth replaced by history (section 23).

The world-historical significance of this defeat of spontaneity was the almost uninterrupted victory of a life divorced from its creative spark. In place of the life-affirming noble, this shift brought with it a humanity characterised by 'abstract man . . .; abstract education, abstract morality; abstract law; the abstract state'. The ripples of this epochal transformation continue to be felt centuries later: 'the present age' is, for Nietzsche, 'the result of that Socratism which is bent on the destruction of myth' (section 23).

Central to Nietzsche's thesis is that the demise of myth and of its expression in tragedy go far beyond the confines of purely 'aesthetic' interest. It reaches into the very essence, heart and nature of 'national life' and 'national character'.

It had to appear to us that the demise of Greek tragedy was brought about through a remarkable and forcible dissociation of these two primordial artistic drives [Dionysus and Apollo]. To this process there corresponded a degeneration and transformation of the character of the Greek people, which calls for serious reflection on how necessary and close the fundamental connections are between art and the people, myth and custom, tragedy and the state.

(Nietzsche, 1967, section 23)

From this perspective, the death of the old tragedy brought about the death of the Greek national character – nobility. Its defeat by Socrates, although himself a member of the noble caste, was symptomatic of the victory of its nemesis, the slave caste. In recognisable terms, Nietzsche has this to say about their intervention onto the world stage:

> There is nothing more terrible than a class of barbaric slaves who have learned to regard their existence as an injustice, and now prepare to avenge, not only themselves, but all generations.[9]

One avenue, or, rather, one person, pointed the way to a potential overcoming of this lifeless existence, Richard Wagner. Wagner's tragedies, Nietzsche predicated, would rip asunder the art and opera that had developed under Socratic influence – abstract, soulless, flippant entertainment – through the unbinding of life from nature, and the renewal of the Dionysian and the Apolline. In what reads as a plot from one of Wagner's own music dramas, Nietzsche presents the figure of Wagner as the Redeemer of the German spirit.

> [N]evertheless in some inaccessible abyss the German spirit still rests and remains undestroyed, in glorious health and profundity, and Dionysian strength, like a knight sunk in slumber; and from this abyss the Dionysian song rises to our ears to let us know that this German knight is still dreaming his primordial Dionysian myth in blissfully serious visions. Let no one believe that the German spirit has forever lost its mythical home where it can still understand so plainly the voices of the birds that tell of that home. Someday it will find itself awake in all the morning freshness following a tremendous sleep: then it will slay dragons, destroy vicious dwarfs, wake Brunnhilde – and even Wotan's spear will not be able to stop its course.
>
> (Nietzsche, 1967, section 24)

Subsumed within this belief in the potential of the rebirth of tragedy is, of course, the rebirth of the noble. The myths and their manner of articulation that defined Wagner's work was intended as an expression of the reincarnation of the pre-Socratic Greek noble. It was only this noble who had the strength and power to stare into the abyss of the terror of human existence, to confront and subsume within himself the god, Dionysus, and not only survive in the face of that knowledge, but render it visible to others through his own Apolline structures.

---

9   Nietzsche, 1967, section 18.

The genealogy of the noble: *On the Genealogy of Morals*

In certain important respects, many of the themes present in *The Birth of Tragedy* remain in *On the Genealogy of Morals*. These include, inter alia, the cultural decadence of contemporary Germany, the absence of life-affirming creativity and the coldness of the triumph of reason and rationality. Yet, it is also the case that these matters are approached from different perspectives. In the present context, however, it is the comparison between the two works and their discussion and evaluation of the noble that is of importance.

In the preface to *On the Genealogy of Morals*, Nietzsche announces the object of his enquiry: the origins and roots of the moral evaluation inherent within the concept 'good'. Approaching this subject-matter genealogically, Nietzsche immediately identifies it as the expression of a given type's will to power.

> It is of no little interest to discover that, in these words and roots which denote 'good', we can often detect the main nuance which made the noble feel they were men of higher rank ... But the names [they adopt for themselves] also show a *typical character trait*: and this is what concerns us here.
>
> (Nietzsche, 2002, section 5)

It is this connection between 'noble' and 'good' that is relevant within the context of Nietzsche's overarching thesis. The two modes of moral evaluation that contain the concept 'good' – good and bad and good and evil – are the products of two distinct character traits or types, the noble and the slave respectively. As Nietzsche develops his ideas, it becomes clear that the concept of the noble is intimately tied to the fate of the concept 'good'; that just as 'good' becomes the product of slave morality, so too the slave becomes the content of the concept 'noble'. Implicit within Nietzsche's argument is the recognition that, just as the slave wilfully inverts his own moral evaluation from evil to good, so the concept of the noble masks its shift of content to the slave.

In the earlier *Birth of Tragedy* it is more the 'objective' product of the noble that is discussed, that is, the nature of myth and tragedy. In the later work, it is the subjective element that Nietzsche depicts. For example, the idea of the cruel beauty and suffering that had infused Nietzsche's earlier account of pre-Socratic Greek culture appears now from the point of view of the noble's subjectivity.

> It was the noble races which left the concept of 'barbarian' in their traces wherever they went; even their highest culture betrays the fact that they were conscious of this and indeed proud of it (for example, when

Pericles, in that famous funeral orientation, tells his Athenians, 'Our daring has forced a path to every land and sea, erecting timeless memorials to itself everywhere for good *and ill*). This 'daring' of the noble races, mad, absurd and sudden in a way it manifests itself, the unpredictability of their undertakings – Pericles singles out the *rayhumia* . . . of the Athenians for praise – their unconcern and scorn for safety, body, life, comfort, their shocking cheerfulness and depth of delight in all destruction, in all the debauches of victory and cruelty – all this, for those who suffered under it, was summed up in the image of the 'barbarian', the 'evil individual', perhaps the 'Goth' or 'Vandal'.
(Nietzsche, 2002, section 11)

A similar pattern emerges when Nietzsche discusses the causes of the noble's demise. In both books its demise is brought about by figures who emerge from the noble caste itself. In each instance, the figures are presented as the expression of the slave caste and the mode of their evaluation.[10] Yet, it is in the discussion of this overcoming of the noble by the slave that the two studies diverge. In the earlier work, it is the figure of Socrates that is central, whilst in the *Genealogy* it is, at least in the majority of the work, the figure of the Priests that predominate. It is only in section 7 that it is the Jews who are attributed this role.

Whilst commentators have reflected on the move from Socrates to Priests, little comment has been made concerning the shift from Priests to the Jews. More often than not, the reduction of the Priests into 'the Jews' tends to be assumed without further comment. To appreciate more fully this latter transition, it is necessary first to return to Nietzsche's relationship and changing evaluation of Wagner and his works; that is, to present this relationship genealogically noting the changes and transformations that occur within the name 'Wagner',[11] a genealogy that is matched by Nietzsche's own attitude toward antisemitism.

From their first meeting, Nietzsche's notebooks and writings contain frequent and increasingly hostile references to Richard Wagner.[12] Prominent amongst these sketches are *Wagner at Bayreuth*, *The Case Against Wagner*, the collection of notes published under the title, *Nietzsche contra Wagner*, as well as sections 2 to 5 of the third essay of the *Genealogy*, 'What do ascetic

---

10 See below.
11 It must be noted in passing, of course, that the venom of Nietzsche's pen is directed not only at Wagner himself, but also the acolytes of the 'Bayreuth idealism' who centred around the *Bayreuth Blatter*. A further target of Nietzsche's polemic was also those 'nobles' of an aryan 'new world' associated with his sister, Elisabeth, and his brother-in-law, Berhard Foster. As is well documented, Nietzsche's attitude to this latter group is one of exasperated irritation and annoyance at the attempts to seek his stamp of approval for their madcap schemes and for their wilful misquotations of his works. See also Yovel, 2002.
12 See Koehler, 1998; Silk and Stern, 1981; Millington, 2000.

ideals mean?' Yet, perhaps the most seething commentary on Wagner that Nietzsche offered is contained in the first essay of the *Genealogy*, 'Good and Bad', 'Good and Evil'. Although no mention is made of Wagner by name, close parallels exist[13] between the genealogy of his type and Nietzsche's depiction of the slave, the man of *ressentiment*.

Despite reservations that remained secreted in his notebooks, *The Birth of Tragedy* looked to Wagner's work as inaugurating a new epoch in which German culture would be reawakened and revitalised, a view that Nietzsche later retracted. As is well documented, Nietzsche broke with 'the Master' shortly after the publication of this first book. Accounts of this split have varied over the years, but there is now general consensus that this parting was hastened by the spectacle of the first Bayreuth festival. Far from reviving the praxis of ancient tragedy that Nietzsche had hoped and Wagner had professed, the nature of that event confirmed the troubling thoughts he had been nursing for some time. In both his personality and his creative works, Nietzsche recognised that Wagner had become 'a representative of the bourgeoisie culture [Nietzsche] so loathed'.[14] Safranski describes the scene that greeted Nietzsche that confirmed his suspicions:

> [Nietzsche] was horrified, and even nauseated to witness the ostentatious arrival of Kaiser Wilhelm I, [Wagner's] fawning demeanour on the festival hill at Wahnfried (the Wagner's villa in Bayreuth), the unintended comicality of the staging, the racket about the mythical enterprise, and the high-spirited, prosperous spectators to this artistic event who were in search not of redemption,[15] but of a good meal.
> (Safranski, 2002, pp 106–7)

Over the ensuing years and culminating in his critique of *Parsifal*,[16] Nietzsche came to realise that the Wagnerian myths (in which he included Wagner's meticulous cultivation of his self-image) were far from representing the potential for an overcoming of what he saw as the decadence of Bismarkian culture. Rather, Nietzsche viewed them as an expression of that culture; a culture Nietzsche defined precisely as one that lacked the noble spirit of its pre-Socratic antecedent. In this process, Nietzsche unmasks Wagner the noble to

---

13 The views expressed by the slave in this essay mirror may of Wagner's writings, old and new, especially those since labelled 'regeneration', as well as those of his circle; see Millington, 2000.
14 Millington, 2000 and Koehler, 1998. See also Mandle, 2001 for a discussion of Nietzsche's attendance at Bayreuth.
15 Safranski also makes the interesting point that where Wagner believed in *redemption* through art, Nietzsche believed in art's power of *transcendence*.
16 Although the centrality of Nietzsche's critique of *Parsifal* has been overstated in recent years. See Millington, 2000.

reveal Wagner the slave; his masquerade a mere, but nonetheless, dangerous pose. This point emerges clearly when section 7 is read through the prism of section 10, Nietzsche's discussion of the nature of *ressentiment*. Before so doing, it is necessary first to place section 7 into the context of the preceding discussion, notably sections 5 and 6.

It is in sections 5 and 6 that Nietzsche develops his genealogical thesis concerning the concept 'good'. He argues that the conflict between the moral evaluations of 'good and bad' and 'good and evil' arose originally as the expression of a conflict within the noble caste itself, that between warrior and priest. As in the *Birth of Tragedy*, Nietzsche is at pains to stress that the outcome of the conflict was the slave's overcoming of the noble. So complete was this victory that the noble, once so powerful, was brought down to the level of the slave.

It is this thesis that in section 7 becomes subject to Nietzsche's striking irony. The tone and content of section 7, both within itself and in relation to the previous sections, imply that the history of the ignoble and irretrievable defeat of the noble has been written by the noble himself. The irony here is that the voice of the ancient noble, defeated centuries earlier, can no longer be heard, at least in the first person. Instead, it can only be the voice of the man of *ressentiment*, the slave, the one who masquerades as the noble. In other words, section 7 offers an account of the practical outcomes of the developments of sections 5 and 6 – the way in which the concepts of 'good' and 'noble' have suffered a shared fate of inverted meaning.

The rather academic explanatory style of sections 5 and 6 is replaced by the boorishness of section 7 through which a bowdlerised and vulgarised version of the same events is repeated. In place of reflection and a certain open-endedness, the reader is suddenly confronted with the crudity and siren of simple assertion. This transition is evidenced by reference to the following two quotes. Despite Nietzsche's aversion to the priestly intervention in history, the section concludes with a sensitive and ambivalent reflection on the place and role of the priest in the trajectory of moral and cultural development.

> Priests make *everything* more dangerous, not just medicaments and healing arts but pride, revenge, acumen, debauchery, love, lust for power, virtue, sickness; – in any case, with some justification one could add that man first became an *interesting animal* on the foundation of this *essentially dangerous* form of human existence, the priest and the human soul became *deep* in the higher sense and turned *evil* for the first time – and of course, these are the two basic forms of man's superiority, hitherto, over other animals!
>
> (Nietzsche, 2002, section 6)

This nuanced and 'objective' account can be compared to the expression of the same point in section 7.

> The history of mankind would be far too stupid a thing if it has not the intellect [*Geist*] of the powerlessness[17] injected into it:– let us take the best example straight away. Nothing which has been done on earth against 'the noble', 'the mighty', 'the masters' and 'the rulers', is worth mentioning compared with what *the Jews* have done against them.
>
> (Nietzsche, 2002, section 7)

In the transition from section 6 to section 7, Nietzsche's undoubtedly severe anti-clericalism and anti-asceticism,[18] which includes a vast span of historical references including that of Brahmanism and Buddhism – and *not*, it is to be noted, Brahmins and Buddhists – is now reduced to one single group, 'the Jews'. In place of evidence of depth and breadth of learning along with nuance of argument and presentation, section 7 speaks of 'the Jews' as if they are the personification of the unrelenting and unending misfortune that has befallen the noble from time immemorial to the present.

This vulgar conception of 'the Jews' can be compared with that of Nietzsche's comments elsewhere in the *Genealogy* as well as his other published works. These other discussions of the Jews emphasise either their 'positive' intercession in world history, or, in more measured and less effusive terms, presents the role of such intervention more in keeping with the tone and content of sections 5 and 6. Again, therefore, the subtlety of thought associated with Nietzsche is replaced by the thuggery of thought identified with the man of *ressentiment*.

Perhaps the most significant clue to the identity of the narrator of section 7 surfaces in the characterisation of the priests, now reduced to that of 'the Jews, that priestly people', as 'the most *evil* enemies'. This 'slip of the tongue' prefigures the concluding comments of Nietzsche's portrait of the man of *ressentiment* in section 10.

> How much respect a noble man has for his enemies! – and a respect of that sort is a bridge to love ... For he insists on having his enemy to himself, as a mark of distinction, indeed, he will tolerate as enemies none other than such as have nothing to be despised and a *great deal* to be honoured! Against this, imagine 'the enemy' as conceived by the man of *ressentiment* – and here we have his deed, his creation: he has conceived of this 'evil enemy', '*the evil one*' as a basic idea to which he now thinks up a copy and counterpart, the 'good one' – himself.
>
> (Nietzsche, 2002, section 10)

---

17 See below.

18 Whilst this point should not be overstated, Wagner's proclaimed respect for Schopenhauer should not be forgotten.

As this quote makes clear, this perception of the Jews as 'the most *evil enemies*' – and the emphasis is Nietzsche's – unequivocally points to its origins within the mind of the slave and not that of the noble. This interpretation is in keeping with the force of Nietzsche's essay: to trace the trajectory of the overcoming of the noble's moral evaluation of 'good and bad' by that of the slave's 'good and evil'.

This *trompe d'oeil* continues when the narrator offers an answer to his own rhetorical question as to why these enemies, their enemies, are evil. The reason preferred is 'because they are the most powerless'. Unable to fight physically, that is, in a noble manner, the Jews are said to undermine their counter-caste through subtle subterfuge. Their very passivity becomes the measure of their strength. Yet, in this outpouring of righteous indignation, the modern noble overlooks his own impotence, his own unwillingness to confront his enemy in a noble way that is open and honourable. Not only does this point illustrate the passivity of this modern noble, but is projected onto their enemies through the prism of moral inversion, in which 'lies are turning weakness into an *accomplishment* . . . and impotence which doesn't retaliate is being turned into goodness' (section 13).

Echoing a point made by the 'noble' himself – that 'out of this powerlessness, their hate swells into something huge and uncanny to a most intellectual and poisonous level' – Nietzsche notes in section 10 that:

> [w]hen *ressentiment* does occur in the noble man himself, it is consumed and exhausted in an immediate reaction, and therefore it does not *poison*, on the other hand, it does not occur at all in countless cases where it is unavoidable for all who are weak and powerless.
>
> (Nietzsche, 2002, section 10)

This effects of this poison are clearly evidenced in the venomous tone of section 7 and the almost absurd claims made by the narrator. These include the figure of the Jew as evil, their bringing down all nobility, their destruction of culture for millennia. This image of 'the Jews' as the destroyer of all noble things, especially its expression in culture,[19] is a prevalent theme amongst the antisemitic canon and is on all fours with the description of the man of *ressentiment's* art of portraiture. It is this crude representation that replaces the nuanced role of the diverse instances of Priestly castes that have existed from Ancient Greece to the present day and which Nietzsche discusses in the previous sections.

This pervasive and obsessive paranoia that is present in this list of accusations brought about by this poisoning is traced by Nietzsche to a further

---

19 It is to be noted that this was one of Wagner's enduring complaints – that the Jews had destroyed German culture (see Millington, 2000).

symptom of a *ressentiment* unable to discharge itself. This symptom expresses itself as a paranoia in which the enemy appears in gigantean and uncanny forms. Paradoxically, this belief in one's own conspiratorial fantasy grants to the slave's adversaries far more power that they in fact possess.

> While the noble man is confident and frank with himself . . . the man of *ressentiment* is neither upright not naïve, nor honest and straight with himself. His soul *squints*; his mind loves dark corners, secret paths and back-doors, everything secretive appeals to him as being *his* world, *his* security, *his comfort*; he knows all about keeping quiet, not forgetting, waiting, temporarily humbling and abasing himself . . . To be unable to take his enemies, his misfortunes and even his *misdeeds* seriously for long – that is the sign of strong, rounded natures with a superabundance of a power which is flexible, formative, healing and can make one forget . . . A man like this shakes from him, with one shrug, many worms which would have burrowed into another man.
> (Nietzsche, 2002, 1:10)

It is at this point that the gap between the ancient and modern noble is most apparent. As noted in the previous section, a prime characteristic of the ancient noble was his ability to live in the knowledge of the terrors of raw nature. The power of the Ancient Greek tragedy, Nietzsche argues, was to articulate that fear without denying its force. Conversely, the modern noble's mythologies act in the opposite way. This mythology of the Jews, a parody of ancient mythology, is created through a spiralling relationship between the modern noble and his own warped and poisoned imagination. The Jews and their imagined power become the *idée fixée*[20] of the modern noble, an idea whose power accumulates with the memory of each and every fictitious slight and injury to their noble sensitivities. The entire world comes to be seen in terms of a hermetic, self-replicating system of conspiracies, secret cabals,[21] all of which ensnare him in their grasp.[22] As such, this paranoid relationship acts as a boundary to the intrusion or recognition of nature's power in the act of creation. Wrapped in a world of its own delusion, the detachment from nature, from what Nietzsche saw as the spark of life-creativity, is almost complete.[23]

---

20 Note the musical origins of this term utilised by Nietzsche.
21 See section 14 for an account of this phenomenon, but this time from the perspective of the 'free-spirit'.
22 It is this point, and the paranoia to which it is connected (see below) that explains the paranoid fantasy that Christianity is a Jewish plot for world domination. See Rose, 1993, pp 89–111 on the historical relationship between Judaism and Christianity and Nietzsche's knowledge of their connections.
23 In painting an image of this type, Nietzsche offers what must rank as one of the finest portraits of the antisemite and his traits.

Nietzsche recognises the nature of this disease of the mind in which self-perpetuating delusions and dark fantasies stand in for the nature of the real world. Again, its cause is the presence of a destructive and dangerous *ressentiment*.

> When the noble method of evaluation makes a mistake and sins against reality, this happens in relation to the sphere with which it is *not* sufficiently familiar, a true knowledge of which it has indeed rigidly resisted: in some circumstances, it misjudges the sphere it despises, that of the common man, the rabble; on the other hand, we should bear in mind that the distortion which results from the feeling of contempt, disdain and superciliousness, always assuming that the image of the despised person is *distorted*, remains far behind the distortion with which the entrenched hatred and revenge of the powerless man attacks his opponent – in effigy of course. Indeed, contempt has too much negligence, nonchalance, complacency and impatience, even too much personal cheerfulness mixed into it, for it to be in a position to transform its object into a real caricature and monster.
>
> (Nietzsche, 2002, 1:10)

The implication of this insight is quite startling. 'The Jews' that appear in section 7 of the first essay of *On the Genealogy of Morals* are 'caricatures' and 'distortions'. They are but 'effigies', their form and substance a product of what Nietzsche saw as deranged and pathological minds. It was only later that the fate that awaits effigies at the hands of their opponents was transferred onto millions of unique and particular individuals.

Conclusion

Whilst it is clear that section 7 of the first essay of the *Genealogy* has nothing to say of Nietzsche's 'attitude' to the Jews, nor offers any sensible account of the development of Judaism over the centuries, it does offer an early insight into the psyche of the antisemite, as well as re-establishing Nietzsche's anti-antisemitic credentials.

In many ways, the portrait that Nietzsche paints of the modern 'noble' is as a parody of his venerable predecessor. Both types, for example, stand in a negative relationship to 'logos', but in a different position. The ancient noble was left behind at reason's dawn, whilst the modern noble confronts the latter at reason's dusk. Correspondingly, whilst the ancients lived in and for the present, their erstwhile successors looked only to the future through a retreat into the past. Put another way, the myths of the ancient Greeks for Nietzsche offered a 'yes' to life, the myth of the antisemite screams out a conformist 'no'; Apollo has secured dominance over a defeated Dionysus.

The nature of the myths each constructed was equally of a different kind. The myth of the pre-Socratic Greeks accepted the contingency of life and the arbitrariness of nature; the antisemitic myth, on the other hand, refused all chance by making the universe amenable to some negative grand design driven by the conscious action of one particular entity, 'the Jews'. Unlike the ancient noble, the modern noble's action is always reaction and one that brings with it the verbiage of moral outrage.

In offering this portrait of the antisemite, Nietzsche can claim the status as one of the first commentators to recognise and criticise the appearance of a social and cultural phenomenon that had only appeared on the scene most recently. This figure of the slave-noble is distinguished from the man of reason and the man of science as well as the old anti-Judaic religious bigot. Yet, despite his perception, it would be wrong to characterise Nietzsche as a prophet heralding the events of the following century. At the time of writing, antisemitism was not the only symptom of cultural exhaustion, nor had it achieved its victory over all other competing 'isms'.[24] Nonetheless, it is equally the case that Nietzsche's genealogy of the noble offers a pessimistic view of the world in which the 'inversions of well-known ideas imply that society has undergone an extremely perverse fate, and has turned into the obverse of its ideals' (Rose, 1978, p 26).[25]

---

24 See Arendt, 1979, p 9.
25 See also Adorno and Horkheimer, 2002.

Chapter 6

The jurisprudence of Nazi monumental architecture

> How can one choose to reason falsely? It is because of a longing for impenetrability. The rational man groans as he gropes for truth; he knows that his reasoning is no more than tentative, that other considerations may supervene to cast doubt on it. He never sees very clearly where he is going; he is 'open'; he may even appear to be hesitant. But there are people who are attracted by the durability of a stone. They wish to be massive and impenetrable; they wish not to change ... It is as if their own existence were in continual suspension. But they wish to exist all at once and right away.
>
> (Sartre, 1995, pp 18–19]

> Anyone looking at our great public edifices who refers to 'Neoclassicism' has failed to understand the essence of our mode of building. This essence lies in the new task ahead, in the new all-embracing purpose in our constructions which are unprecedented in their ground-plan, spational layout and integrated shape, and which derive exclusively from the spirit of National Socialist life.
>
> (R Wolters, 1944)[1]

> 'The Buildings of the movement are heroic, which accords with their very essence' ... And this 'heroic architecture' where 'the criterion of the individual ... gives way ... to that of the military unit and whose organic formation' ... reflects the disciplined marching of the columns takes up aesthetic models wherever they seem likely to suggest 'grandeur and monumentality'.
>
> (N Stephan, 1939)[1]

Introduction

A striking aspect of Nazi monumental architecture is its neoclassical style. This style has been explained in a variety of ways. It could be seen as

---

1 Quoted in Schache, 1968.

expressing the domination of reason from the ancient world to the present, a view supported by its similarity to other parts of Europe and North America. But these comparisons play down the vital differences that existed between the national socialist regime and those of liberal or welfare democracies.[2]

Alternatively, Alex Scobie argues that the Nazi reproduction of classical styles represents an attempt to:

> Establish architectural order ... on a scale intended to reinforce the social and political order desired by the Nazi state, which anticipated the displacement of Christian religion and ethical values by a new kind of worship based on the cult of Nazi martyrs and leaders, and with a value system close to that of pre-Christian Rome ... [a] 'Roman' ethics which recognised the natural right of a conqueror to enslave conquered peoples in the most literal sense of the word, a right already made manifest even within the sphere of architecture by the creation of concentration camps, whose inmates were forced to quarry the stone for the Reich's buildings.[3]
> (Scobie, 1990, p 137)

Scobie's view is important. Nazi monumental architecture did hark back to the classical era, but it was to Greek rather than Roman classicism. The idea that pre-Christian Rome can be understood as a precedent for Nazism is also questionable. Finally, the Nazis' aping of the classical style is unintentionally parodic.

In this case, parody arises when the *ressentiment* of the superfluous try to remake a world in their own distorted image. It is a new world that appears to transcend all the contradictions that plagued the old world that rejected them and gave rise to their contemporary condition of superfluousness. In this act of 'creation', Nazism's self-image was that of the nobles of the classical era, especially of those of pre-Socratic Greece. For philosophers such as Heidegger and the young Nietzsche, that era was characterised as one of fabulous creation and expressing harmony between cosmos, nature and humanity. It was an era that they believed was destroyed by logos, by reason and, in some instances, by the Jews.

In the third section of *Origins of Totalitarianism*, Hannah Arendt asks a fundamental question concerning totalitarianism's human foundations:

> If [the unprecedented nature of totalitarianism] is true, then the entirely

---

2   Van Pelt and Westfall, 1993.
3   I find the use of the word 'even' in this quote quite interesting. It is as if there is a gasp of surprise that '*even architecture*', and, by implication, architects can in some way be implicated in Nazism. One can hear the same surprise when it is pointed out that even law and lawyers, medicine and medical staff, sociology and sociologists, philosophy and philosophers, and so on, can also be tainted.

new and unprecedented forms of totalitarian organisation and course of action must rest on one of the few basic experiences which men can have whenever they live together, and are concerned with public affairs. If there is a basic experience which finds its political expression in totalitarian domination, then in view of the novelty of the totalitarian form of government, this must be the experience which, for whatever reason, has never before served as the foundation of a body politic and whose general mood – although it may be familiar in every other respect – never before has pervaded, and directed the handling of, public affairs.

(Arendt, 1979, p 461)

That novel foundation is 'superfluousness'. For Arendt, superfluousness is the result of a process that began in 1914 with the outbreak of the First World War and continued with the political, social and economic catastrophes in its aftermath. It was accelerated and radicalised by totalitarianism. Human superfluousness arises when those 'who have no place in the world, recognised and guaranteed by others' are finally placed in the situation of 'not belong[ing] to the world at all' (Arendt, 1979, p 475).

The superfluous then come to identify themselves with the nobles of the classical era and express that identity in all ways, including through their architecture. As Nietzsche illustrated in his critique of morality, a single word or concept is susceptible to multiple meanings. These meanings, he argued, are expressions of equally diverse wills (2002, pp 11–13). He illustrated this point with the genealogy of the concept of 'good': when paired in one instance with the 'bad', the expression of a noble will to power, and at another instance, when paired with 'evil', an expression of a slavish will, that is, a will to power given substance through *ressentiment*. By analogy, the classicism of Nazi monumental architecture can be unmasked as a parody of the classical era that it claimed as its precedent, an era defined by a seeming connection between humanity and nature. It is, moreover, a parody that unmasks Nazi 'nobility' as the product of the slave and so of the herd or mass.[4]

Ressentiment underpins the forced reconciliation of nature and humanity that simultaneously undermines it. An expression of *ressentiment* is the desire not to be and to abrogate one's subjectivity. As Nietzsche notes, 'man prefers to will nothingness than not will' (2002, p 128). This is the paradox of *ressentiment: that the denial of subjectivity is itself a product of subjectivity*. The greatest desire not to be entails the greatest expenditure of will. The *ressentiment* that is expressed in Nazi monumental architecture which underpins the desire of the masses' subsumption into nature is forever undermined by the subjectivity of that very desire. In this way, *ressentiment* functions not only as

---

4 For an extended discussion of this point, see Chapter 5.

a critique of Nazi monumental architecture, but also of those critics who treat the foundations of Nazism as premised upon the destruction of subjectivity.

The parody of the laws of nature: law without laws

In a manner that recollects Nietzsche's account of the genealogy of the moral valuation of 'good', Arendt traces the way in which the term 'law' changed its meaning. Law began as an expression of the framework of stability within which human actions and movement can take place. It changed to become the expression of movement itself (Arendt, 1979, p 464). The following discussion traces the nature of this transformation as well as the transformation of nature implied within it.

According to Nietzsche, the noblest of all traits exhibited by the nobles of pre-Socratic Greece was their ability to meld the Dionysian with the Apolline. In this way, the terrifying and potentially destructive power of nature was mitigated. The result brought into existence what many have considered to be the most sublime and the noblest of aesthetic eras. It was this nobility that Nazism inverted and parodied.

For Hannah Arendt and Adorno and Horkheimer, writing during and in the immediate aftermath of national socialism, Nazism was treated as coming into existence precisely as an expression of humanity's increasing exclusion from nature. They also note that it was at this very moment of ejection that the idea of an unmediated nature came to predominate. Whereas for the ancient Greeks, the terror of nature was mediated by human fabrication, Nazism channelled the terror of its false nature into its own aim. That aim was to make the superfluous truly fit for their own fate in the service of domination.

Unlike Greek Dionysian nature, characterised by its absence of meaning and direction, Nazism's parody of nature turns it into vengeful legislation. Now cast as the 'law of nature', judgements are freed from the restraint of human reflection and positivist expression. This law of nature eschews every aspect of its human subject. Its judgements of nature are 'always already' made. In this way:

> [t]otalitarian lawfulness, defying legality and pretending to establish the direct reign of justice on earth, executes the law of History or of Nature without translating it into the standards of right and wrong for individual behaviour. It applies the law directly to mankind without bothering with the behaviour of men . . . Totalitarian policy claims to transform the human species into an active unfailing carrier of a law to which human beings would only passively and reluctantly be subjected.
>
> (Arendt, 1979, p 462)

Nazism's underlying superfluousness thus expresses itself in the guise of nature and law. By denying the Apolline – the human artifice and positive law – Nazism and the authority of its rule of the law of nature renders all subjective attributes superfluous. As a parody of nature, this alleged law of nature is in fact an inversion of the relationship between humanity, nature and the cosmos that defined ancient Greek culture and which gave rise to the nobility of its age. More specifically, the law of nature inverts the relationship between the restless movement of nature and the stability of society.

> This identification of man and law ... has nothing in common with the *lumen naturale* or the voice of conscience, by which Nature or Divinity as the sources of authority for the *ius naturale* or the historically revealed comments of God are supposed to announce their authority. This never made man a walking embodiment of the law, but on the contrary remained distinct from him as the source of authority that demanded consent and obedience. Nature and Divinity as the source of authority for positive laws were thought of as permanent and eternal; positive laws were changing and changeable according to circumstances, but they possessed a relative permanence as compared with the much more rapidly changing actions of men; and they derived this permanence from the eternal presence of their source of authority. Positive laws, therefore, are primarily designed to function as stabilizing factors for the ever-changing movements of men.
> (Arendt, 1979, p 463)

Since subjectivity is an irrelevance to the laws of nature's pre-ordained findings, the role of human institutions is to be nothing other than executors – or executioners – of its eternal will. As a consequence, the human reflection that mediated traditional natural law and its judgements is substituted by terror.

> Terror executes the judgements, and before its court, all concerned are subjectively innocent: the murdered because they did nothing against the system and the murderers because they do not really murder but execute a death sentence pronounced by some higher tribunal. The rulers themselves do not claim to be just or wise; they do not apply laws, but execute a movement in accordance with its inherent law. Terror is lawfulness, if law is the law of movement of some suprahuman force, Nature or History.
> (Arendt, 1979, p 465)

For Arendt, the 'objectivity' inherent within this suprahuman law of nature not only marks who shall die, but also who shall be executioners. 'Nature itself decided, not only who was to be eliminated, but also who was to be trained as an executioner' (1979, p 468). In this apparently objective situation in which all live in fear, but in which fear is no guide to survival, no one is safe. It is quite possible – indeed, it is necessary – for the constant movement brought about by the law of nature and the terror of its processes that the executioner of today can quite easily be the victim of tomorrow.

> The inhabitants of a totalitarian country are thrown into and caught in the process of nature or history for the sake of accelerating the movement; as such, they can only be executioners or victims of its inherent law. The process may decide that those who today eliminate races and individuals or members of dying classes and decadent peoples are tomorrow those who must be sacrificed. What totalitarian rule needs to guide the behaviour of its subjects is a preparation to fit each of them equally well for the role of the executioner and role of victim.
> (Arendt, 1979, p 468)

And, here, the superfluousness of humanity becomes most obvious. Humanity exists as a mass of future dead[5] to be sacrificed at the alter of a slavish parody of the recreation of an ancient, noble world.

This reading of Nazism has emphasised its slavish imitation of classical nobility. It is equally the case, though, that Nazism's law of nature is as much informed by a *ressentiment* against a modern notion of rights as it is by a nostalgia for the past. Consider, for example, Nazism's desire to be rid of the responsibilities associated with social existence as a rights-bearing individual manifested by dissolution into the herd or mass.[6] Consider also Nazism's belief in a law of nature that aims at the 'fabrication of mankind' in which 'individuals [are eliminated] for the sake of the species, [as] sacrifices for the sake of the whole' (Arendt, 1979, p 465). In place of autonomy and plurality guaranteed by rights and laws, Nazism's law of nature creates the 'one man of gigantic dimensions'.

> By pressing men against each other, total terror destroys the space between them . . . Totalitarian government does not just curtail liberties or abolish essential freedoms; nor does it, at least to our limited knowledge, succeed in eradicating the love for freedom from the hearts of man. It destroys the one essential prerequisite of all freedom that is simply the capacity of motion that cannot exist without space.
> (Arendt, 1979, p 466)

Arendt's imagery evokes Nazism's forced reconciliation of humanity and nature: the petrifaction of man takes on the character of the petrifaction of

---

5 In *Essays in Understanding* Arendt refers to camp inmates as the 'already dead' (1994, p 236). The reference here to *future* dead refers to those who comprise the general population inside as well as outside the camp.
6 See generally on this point Chapter 4.

nature. Compressed into one solid mass, man becomes nature, but it is the dead nature of those excluded from the world. Man and nature both become as stone. Within this petrified mass, where any particle can be exchanged for any other, nothing of living humanity remains. Like petrified nature, 'man' has become truly superfluous.

As compelling as this account of Nazism is, it overlooks one essential point. The creation of the alternative dead world is a product of a law of nature in appearance only. Excluded from the world, it is the superfluous who create its parody. It is not Dionysus who wreaks the terror of its judgements, but Apollo, set free from the constraints and terror of real nature.

Consider in this light the first 'authentic' decrees said to be determined from the Nazi law of nature. In the mid–1930's, when national socialism was consolidating its stranglehold on German society, it passed the Nuremberg 'race' laws and the law relating to 'health' (the beginnings of the sterilisation and euthanasia programmes). The obvious irrationality and superfluousness of these measures (neither Jews nor the ill posed any sort of threat to the Nazis, or to the political and social life of Germany)[7] are presented as 'rationality' and 'necessity'. The superfluousness of these decrees already spoke of the superfluousness of those it named. As Arendt notes, not only was superfluousness not confined to 'the Jews', it could also encompass any other 'objective' category, real or imagined.[8] Importantly, it is also at this time that the Nazi monumental architectural project began in earnest.[9]

The Nazi parody of classical monumental architecture: 'noble' without nobility

If, as Hitler stated, architecture is the 'word in stone', then nowhere does the word express itself more clearly than in Nazi monumental architecture. The *ressentiment* that makes the superfluous necessary, the slave the noble, the Apolline the Dionysian and terror as politics, is expressed in its building, aesthetics and performative aspects. Nazi monumental architecture was ripped from any connection with rational social functions.

---

7 Arendt, 1994.
8 Arendt's point here is not the dissolution of 'the Jews' under a generic category of totalitarianism but that the very nature of totalitarianism demanded the ceaseless finding of other groups to share the same fate as the Jews. For Arendt, antisemitism constituted a central and invariable element within Nazism: 'Many still consider it an accident that Nazi ideology centred around antisemitism and that Nazi policy, consistently and uncompromisingly, aimed at the persecution and finally the extermination of the Jews ... The point for the historian is that the Jews, before becoming the main victims of terror, were the centre of Nazi ideology' (Arendt, 1979, pp 3, 7).
9 Arendt (1994) speaks of Germany being completely pacified by 1934 at the earliest and 1936 at the latest.

Along with the desire to impress, Nazi monumental architecture was also intended to act as propaganda. Something of this function is indicated in Goebbels' sycophantic[10] diary entry of late 1937, in which he makes the connection between conquest and architecture.

> The Führer really loves Berlin. The more he gets to know it the more attached he becomes. Discussions with Speer about building projects . . . Austria and Czechoslovakia. We must have both of these to round off our territory. And we will get them. When their citizens come to Germany, they are bowled over by our size and power. These little countries have a pathetic sense of their own greatness. But when their people come to Germany they are simply bowled over by the size and power of the Reich. We need to emphasize this more. It is the reason for the Führer's gigantic building project.
>
> (quoted in Spotts, 2002, p 330)[11]

Note the *ressentiment* that permeates the writing. Note also the accuracy of Goebbels' comments. Recognising this accuracy, Arendt observes that the totalitarian use of propaganda is aimed less at the internal population than at the non-totalitarian world. This point is particularly interesting considering that the monumental architecture programme began in earnest precisely at the moment that the Nazis had consolidated their powers, when the need for persuasion had been substituted by the reign of terror[12] (Arendt, 1979, p 344).

From this perspective their potential as propaganda cannot explain entirely the aesthetics and functions of these buildings. They are equally important as expressions of Nazi 'legality', that vengeful Law of Nature executing its will in a world constructed within its terrifying domain. Now the superfluousness of architecture coincides with an architecture of superfluousness.

The Law for the Redesign of German Cities was decreed in 1937 and Albert Speer was appointed Inspector General for Building in Berlin. Speer became 'accountable only to Hitler' and his 'administrative entity separate from both party and state' (Jaskot, 2000, p 85). Thus, along with the police, the true instruments of totalitarianism and terror,[13] and the concentration

---

10 Reading the diaries of Nazis and other contemporaries, one is constantly surprised at their sycophantic tone. Quite apart from the fact that many did admire Hitler, it is equally the case that they seemed to believe that even their most reflective moments were visible and that their most intimate thoughts, already known, so to speak, could be used against them at any given moment. Of course, such sycophancy spared no-one. Nothing quite expresses Arendt's point on the loss of solitude within totalitarianism.

11 This reference to 'visitors' should not, of course, exclude the propagandist effect these buildings would have on Germany's own population.

12 'The point of it all [was to leave everyone] overwhelmed or, rather, stunned [at the power and majesty of the Reich]' (Speer, quoted in Spotts, 2002, p 359).

13 Arendt, 1979, p 289.

camps under their control, the superfluous necessity of monumental buildings became the institutional expression of power.

> The gigantic organization of public works ... was created by Hitler outside all party hierarchies and affiliations. This organisation might have been used against the authority of party or even police organizations. It is noteworthy that Speer could risk pointing out to Hitler (during a conference in 1942) the impossibility of organising production under Himmler's regime, and even demand jurisdiction over slave labour and concentration camps.
> (Arendt, 1979, footnote 39, p 402)[14]

In his outstanding study, Jaskot (2000) notes that this decree was passed at the same time as decrees stating that 'Aryans' made homeless by the land-clearing necessitated by the Nazi monumental building plan were to be rehoused in dwellings emptied of their Jewish tenants, thereby denying Jews their property and legal rights. Jaskot makes the telling point that, far from an ad hoc response to a particular logistical 'problem', the SS and GBI[15] (under Speer's direct command) took into account the 'need' to 'concentrate' Berlin's Jews. This association of law, terror and building plans continued throughout the war years. In a memorandum of 1941, Speer records that:

> [a]bout two years ago, the Furher had placed Jewish housing under my disposal for my 'demolition tenants' and around August of that year ordered on my recommendation that housing blocks which were designed to be cleared [for the building] should be cleared already during the war. The use of the available Jewish dwellings and empty housing should be kept ready for families rendered temporarily homeless through bomb damage.
> (Jaskot, 2000, p 101)

At the time this note was written, unlike five years earlier when Jews were rehoused, these (unnamed) occupants of 'Jewish housing' and 'Jewish dwellings' were transported immediately to the death camps.

The terror of Nazi totalitarianism expressed within its monumental architecture does not cease at the clearing of 'superfluous' peoples. In both their

---

14 For a discussion of the Party's inner conflicts over architecture, the control of concentration camps and so exploitable labour, see Jaskot, 2000.
15 The GBI was an SS front that bullied and bribed its way into the dominant position in the monumental building economy through its unlimited exploitation of 'superfluous' people and their labour (not, it is to be noted, their labour-*power*). It is also interesting to observe that, in reaching and sustaining this position, the SS destroyed the livelihoods of many small scale 'Aryan' artisans and small businesses (see Jaskot, 2000).

aesthetic and performative dimensions, Nazi monuments express the very 'legality' of Nazi totalitarianism. They express the vengefulness of the Law of Nature, the terror of its suprahuman judgements and the transformations of whole populations into a mass of the superfluous through which each individual becomes exchangeable as victim or executioner.

To sum up thus far, rather than 'neoclassical', Nazi monumental architecture is a parody of classicism in the same way that the Nazi Law of Nature is a parody of natural law. Whereas classical Palladian architecture sought to express the balance existing between the cosmos, nature and 'man', Nazi monumentalism expresses a slave (Apollo) masquerading as a noble (Dionysus). The result is a 'noble' monument bereft of nobility. Something of the nature of this parody is hinted at in Spotts' depiction of such monuments.

> And what [Hitler] wanted was monumental state structures – put another way, structures that were monuments – in neoclassical style. At various times Hitler identified the qualities he sought – 'greatness of conception', 'clarity of plan' and 'harmony of proportion'. While these were unexceptional principles, the treatment he imposed on them – germanische Tektonic, he called it – produced a result that was brutal and cold.
>
> (Spotts, 2002, p 335)

This reference to the brutality of Nazi monuments offers an aesthetic expression of the essence of Nazi totalitarianism. Far from expressing harmony, their sheer size and scale and their granite façades express a brutal overcoming of nature. Nature is made to suffer and yield to their sheer density. Scale and conceit merge into one. The driving force for this parody of classicism was the crudity of mass, bulk and size. It was Hitler's and Speer's obsessive insistence that these monuments overwhelm their noble progenitors no matter the aesthetic or practical cost,[16] and, in turn, speaks of its slavish genesis.

In his study of Hitler's aesthetic tendencies, Frederic Spotts refers to the Viewer Stand for the Zeppelin Field at Nuremberg as 'one of the most emblematic of Third Reich buildings'. To a large extent he is correct. The *ressentiment* of its own period is apparent in its modernist aspects whilst its slave-like parody of classical style is also readily apparent in its dimensions of 1300 feet in length and 80 feet in height. For Spotts, buildings such as this one are characteristic of an 'overriding trait ... of uniformity' in which 'no expression of variety or individuality was tolerated' (Spotts, 2002, p 337).[17]

---

16 Spotts, 2002, p 357.
17 Likewise, Schache (1968) notes in a comment on the Ethnological Museum, a building not dissimilar to the Viewer Stand: 'Although structurally antique elements are incorporated (Doric columns, triglyphic frieze, etc.), these are distorted by scale and proportion until they become unrecognizable ... Its inhuman outsize scale demotes the "Doric columns" of the arcades to the rank of puny architectural pawns which can only make any impact when

The overall effect – and, indeed, intent – was to aggrandize [Hitler] and to debase human beings into tiny subjects, automatons as insensate as the stone of the building.

(Spotts, 2002, p 336)

Spotts' description of this monumental architecture's aesthetics is applicable equally to those who were to populate it at its moments of performance. In the Nuremberg viewing stand, the mass of the superfluous meld with the mass of the architecture and with the mass that comprise the spectacle to be viewed. Presented in this way, it is far from a coincidence that such displays were referred to as 'mass rallies', or, more accurately, rallies of the masses.

The parodic nature of classical aesthetics is matched by the parodic nature of the performance. In these parodies of Greek Dionysian theatre, actor and spectator became entranced and fused in the appearance of the god. The mass of spectators, the mass of participants and the mass of the architecture fuse together to express, in a flash, the seemingly transcendent Law of Nature and the terrifying arbitrariness of is pre-determined judgements. Like the architecture in which all difference is destroyed, it is, for that one moment, as if:

all of humanity were just one individual [and that] each and every person can be reduced to a never-changing identity of reactions, so that each of these bundles can be exchanged at random for any other.

(Arendt, 1979, p 438)

In those moments where objective determination and arbitrary execution merge, one stood suspended never really knowing one's role. In the spectacle of the mass, the mass becomes the embodiment of the true nature of their superfluousness. In the flash of the moment the fate of the superfluous, both executioner and victim, becomes apparent. In this fleeting expression of their superfluousness those present become part of the fantasy of their own necessity. This fantasy, however, can be fuelled only by a denial of subjectivity that can only be achieved by the exercise of subjectivity infused with *ressentiment*. They that would rather will nothing than not will at all.

If the propaganda of truth fails to convince the average person because it is too monstrous, it is positively dangerous to those who know from their

strung together. For the sake of a predominant monumentality, deriving from sheer bulk and volume, and aiming in effect to discipline and intimidate, the structure has been brutally coarsened and the individuality of detail nullified. The monolithic mass transmits into an aura of immutability designed to force the individual into line with the arrayed masses. This would have been the only way of entering into a viable relationship with this architecture. The suppression of the lone architectural feature complemented the social suppression of the individual.'

own imaginings what they themselves are capable of doing and who are, therefore, perfectly willing to believe in the reality of what they have seen. Suddenly, it becomes evident that things which for thousands of years the human imagination had banished to a realm beyond human competence can be manufactured right here on earth, that Hell and Purgatory, and even a shadow of their perpetual duration, can be established by the most modern methods of destruction and therapy. To the people (and they are more numerous in any large city than we like to admit) the totalitarian hell proves only that the power of man is greater than they ever dared to think, and that man can realise hellish fantasies without making the sky fall or the earth open.

(Arendt, 1979, p 466)

For all the terror of these spectacles, it was from the situation of the 'always already' guilty that the true force of the Law of Nature became most apparent. It was a truth expressed through the jurisprudence of Nazi monumental architecture.

The Nazi parody of slavery: slaves without nobles

If the Nazi Law of Nature is an Apolline parody of the natural forces of Dionysus and its monuments that express it are a parody of classicism, then the concentration camp – emerging as a central institution at the same time, the mid–1930s – is a Nazi parody of slavery. To the 'nobles' who saw themselves as the successors to the conquerors of antiquity, the camps' inmates appeared as vanquished and conquered peoples. The Nazis often referred to these detainees as 'slaves' and those with 'slave-like souls'. And the use to which many of them were put, the production of raw materials for public monuments, correspondingly parodies the classical era.

Yet, just as the appropriation of the classical style of monumental architecture contains within it the modernity it was seeking to escape, so the parody of slavery is peppered by an equal dose of *ressentiment* against central concepts of modern law. Unlike the vanquished of the past who were enslaved because of the fact of their defeat,[18] Nazism held their 'slaves' 'guilty' according to the operations of their own 'law'. Their 'guilt' was the product of a judgement of the impersonal and suprahuman law and the camps were the sight of its execution. In fact, the Hell-like terror of the camps can be explained, at least partly, by the 'good conscience' of this *ressentiment*, brought about by the belief that they were only acting according to transcendent dictates (Arendt, 1979, p 445).

---

18 Arendt, 1994, pp 233–4.

It would be a grave mistake, however, to take the word of this 'noble' at face value and to believe that, as much as the slaves were masquerading as nobles, the 'real' nobles had been turned into slaves.[19] Such a romantic and misplaced image overlooks the fact that the inmates' guilt was found without any reference to their actions. In a world where one's fate turned on a mixture of objective determination and arbitrary caprice, there is little that separates those on the inside from those on the outside. Inside the camps, the judgement of superfluousness, passed by the superfluous, was felt through a never-ceasing subjection to the absolute terror of its operations.

> Throughout history slavery has been an institution within a social order; slaves were not, like concentration camp inmates, withdrawn from the sight and hence the protection of their fellow-men; as instruments of labour they had a definite price and as property a definite value. The concentration-camp inmate has no price, because he can always be replaced; nobody knows to whom he belongs, because he is never seen. From the point of view of normal society he is absolutely superfluous, although in times of acute labour shortage . . . he is useful for work.
>
> (Arendt, 1979, p 444)

It is interesting to note the extent to which Arendt's discussion of the concentration camp mirrors that of the nature and jurisprudence of Nazi monumental architecture.

> [I]t is not only the non-utilitarian character of the camps themselves – the senselessness of 'punishing' completely innocent people, the failure to keep them in a condition so that profitable work might be extorted from them, the superfluousness of frightening a completely subdued population – which gives them their distinctive and disturbing qualities, but their anti-utilitarian function, the fact that not even the supreme emergencies of military activities were allowed to interfere with these 'demographic policies'.
>
> (Arendt, 1994, p 233)

The demarcation between executioner and victim was as confused in the camp as it was in the monumental architecture of the mass rallies. At any given moment a 'loyal' party member could find him or herself in the position of the (irredeemable) enemy. Similarly, the hierarchy of functions through which the camps was administered, and in which 'the prisoners did not fail to

---

19 This mistake is most often present in those works which place the ethical bonus onto various entities such as the 'Other' (Levinas), 'the jews' (Lyotard) and the 'refugee' (Agamben). See Rose, 1992 and 1993; Seymour, 2004.

fulfil the same "duties" as the guards themselves' also mirrored the confusion between participants and spectators (Arendt, 1994, p 239).

Taken together these correspondences are expressions of a more general and generic similarity. Both manifest the overarching goal of 'total domination'. Total domination meant the destruction of the humanity that, prior to Nazism, was unthinkable that it could be separable from 'man'. It is worth quoting Arendt at length on this point.

> The supreme goal of all totalitarian governments is not only the freely admitted, long-range ambition to global rule but also to the never-admitted and immediately realized attempt at total domination of man. The concentration camps are the laboratories in the experiments of total domination, for human nature being what it is, this goal can be achieved only under the extreme circumstances of a human-made hell. Total domination is achieved when the human person, who somehow is always a specific mixture of spontaneity and being conditioned, has been transformed into a completely conditioned being whose reactions can be calculated even when he is led to certain death. This disintegration of personality is carried through in difference stages, the first being the moment of arbitrary arrest when the judicial person is being destroyed, not because of the injustice of the arrest but because the arrest stands in no connection whatsoever with the actions or opinions of the person. The second stage of destruction concerns the moral personality and is achieved through the separation of concentration camps from the rest of the world, a separation which makes martyrdom senseless, empty, and is brought about through the permanence and institutionalizing of torture. The end result is the reduction of human beings to the lowest possible denominator of 'identical reactions'.
>
> (Arendt, 1994, p 240)

Arendt here comes close to the belief that the camps really did succeed in their totalitarian goal. Arendt implies that the natural world exists autonomously, as if impervious to the loss of its humanity that had hitherto dwelt within it. As a result, the fate of nature under totalitarianism remains uninvestigated. She need not, therefore, examine the question of labour, human confrontation or engagement with the natural world. Had she done so, however, she would have been able to complete the circle of the fantastical hubris that is the ideal of both the superfluous and of totalitarianism. In both, the ideal is of a 'world' that is fully and utterly malleable and incapable of an autonomous existence. In the idealism of totalitarianism, the superfluousness of humanity would merge with the superfluousness of nature.

This lacuna, which perhaps is a consequence of Arendt's *political* thought, is remedied somewhat by Adorno and Horkheimer's more *social* theory. They emphasise the change that occurs to both humanity and nature in the relationship that exists between them. Driven by the desire to dominate nature,[20] humanity comes increasingly to resemble what it dominated. The essence of this false reconciliation between humanity and nature is the suppression of all spontaneity, human or natural. Reduced to a series of 'brute facts', humanity and nature are denied their inherent uniqueness and unpredictability. They become superfluous.

In the concentration camps[21] earmarked for the 'production' of granite, for example, a superfluous and 'already dead' humanity melded with a superfluous and 'already dead' nature. Granite (the substantive material from which Nazi monumental architecture was to be constructed) is emblematic of this petrifaction. It is created through the fusion of a plurality of elements at extremely high temperatures. As petrified or dead nature – superfluous nature – it mirrors the superfluousness and petrifaction of humanity.

> The iron band of terror, which destroys the plurality of men and makes out of the many the One who will unfailingly act as though he himself were part of the course of history or nature.
>
> (Arendt, 1979, p 466)

> We know that the iron band of total terror leaves no space for . . . private life and the self-coercion of totalitarian logic destroys man's capacities for experience and thought just as certainly as his capacity for action.
>
> (Arendt, 1979, p 474)

Even in the hell of the camps, however, the world Nazism sought to destroy persisted. The camps took a leading role in the provision of granite for Nazi monuments. Jaskot argues that the obscene profits permitted by the use of forced labour provided the motivation to SS involvement.[22] Transformation into the material which they worked is not immediate to the inmate. It depends, as Adorno and Horkheimer suggest, upon a conscious act of will through which the cost of survival is the sacrifice of one's humanity. And, as Primo Levi and Claude Lanzmann remind us, this conscious act was taken over and over again.[23]

---

20 See Adorno and Horkheimer, 2002, and Chapter 2 above.
21 Here, it is worth noting that Arendt's discussion of the concentration camps does not fully demarcate their difference from the death camps. It is the case also that Jaskot's comments on the role of the camps in the building trade questions whether Arendt, as with others, confuses the claims of Nazism for its empirical reality.
22 Jaskot makes the point that, with this involvement, the SS brought financial ruin to many of the independent artisans who believed in their claim to curb the power of 'big business' and unregulated profit.
23 Amongst the many examples the film brings to mind, the one clearest in my mind is of the inmate who, in stealing the shoes of another prisoner, knew not only that he would live, but also that the other would die.

Conclusion: the parody of reconciliation

The Great Hall remained unbuilt. It was designed by Wilhelm Kries to form the centrepiece of a cluster of buildings 'dedicated to death' in the redevelopment of Berlin or 'Germanica'. In its aesthetics, its building materials and its functions, it expresses the parodic reconciliation between humanity and nature that was the hallmark of the Nazi Law of Nature, its terror and its monumental architecture.

The Great Hall offers a clear example of the slavish *ressentiment* masquerading as nobility that pervaded Nazi totalitarianism. Its gigantean dimensions, culminating in a dome reaching 290 metres into the sky undermined its commitment to classical style,[24] and mocked antiquity's reconciliation of nature and humanity.[25] Instead, the Great Hall offered on an even greater scale than the Viewer Stand at Nuremberg the melding of the mass with the architecture.

And, again, we see granite as the construction material of choice. The walls themselves thus express the reconciliation of a petrified nature and a petrified humanity.

But it is in the function of this monument that Nazism's parodic reconciliation of humanity and nature is most evident. A unique feature of the Great Hall was that it was to be built not only as a memorial to past military heroes (including, incidentally, Frederick the Great), but also 'to honour those who would in the future be killed'. In the parody of reconciliation that infuses the Nazi Law of Nature, the entire mass becomes the 'future dead'. The building expresses the judgement of nature that renders through terror the mass as always already dead. What distinguishes this parodic expression from that of the 'Law of Nature' and the concentration camps is the overt confrontation of the population with their own superfluousness. The irony is, of course, that the parodic nature of this reconciliation believed by both totalitarianism and its critics to bring about the destruction of the subject is only possible through the greatest concerted act of those who would rather 'will nothing than not will itself'.

---

24 Schache, 1968.
25 It is in this context that the belief that the sheer size, scale and amount of bodies it could hold would mean it could create its own eco-system, takes on a different dimension.

Chapter 7

Conclusion: Hannah Arendt – the genealogy of antisemitism

It was in the immediate shadow of the Holocaust that Hannah Arendt addressed the question of antisemitism and developed an understanding of it that stands apart from many of the themes present in the works discussed in this study.

First, she was critical of what she termed theories of 'eternal antisemitism' which maintain that from time immemorial (or at least since the birth of Christianity) Jews have always been hated and persecuted by Gentiles and that there was accordingly nothing radically new about this latest outburst. This way of addressing the question, she argued, ignores the determinate character of modern, political antisemitism and its difference from all previous forms of antisemitism.

Second, she was critical of 'scapegoat' theories which ignore the question of 'why the Jews?' in favour of a general theory of the need for, or functions of, scapegoating. This way of understanding antisemitism, she argued, was incapable of addressing the specificity of Jews as victims of extermination. She looked to an approach in which Jews cease to be the 'innocent victim whom the world blames for all its sins' and become instead 'one group of people among other groups, all of whom are involved in the business of this world' (1979, p 6). She emphasises human responsibility, including Jewish responsibility, for antisemitism. Thus, the Jews do not cease to be co-responsible simply because they become victims of the world's injustice.

Third, she was critical of 'victimisation' theories which focus exclusively on the antisemite without taking into account the agency and actions of Jews themselves. These theories, she argued, can only treat Jews as objects of history, never as its purposeful and responsible subjects, and imply the 'complete innocence' of the victims in a way that denies Jews their own role in human history.

Fourth, Arendt was critical of theories of antisemitism, sometimes put forward by antisemites themselves, which explain it as the product of the undue political influence or monetary wealth of Jews. Drawing on an observation made by de Tocqueville, Arendt argued that at no time is a group more vulnerable than when they suffer a 'rapid loss of real power not accompanied by any considerable decline in their fortunes' (1979, p 4). It is at this point, when wealth is dissociated from power, de Tocqueville argued in relation to the French aristocracy, that a previously tolerated group is viewed with particular resentment.

> Neither oppression nor exploitation as such is ever the main cause for resentment; wealth without visible function is much more intolerable because nobody can understand why it should be tolerated.
> (Arendt, 1979, p 4)

Arendt argued that antisemitism followed similar lines: the Jews were attacked most when they had lost their special political functions vis-à-vis the old nation states.

> The remarkable similarity of arguments and images which time and again were spontaneously reproduced have an intimate relationship with the truth they distort. We find the Jews always represented as an international trade organisation, a world-wide family concern with identical interests everywhere, a secret force behind the throne that degrades all visible governments into mere facade, or into marionettes whose strings are manipulated from behind the scenes. Because of their close relationship to state sources of power, the Jews were invariably identified with power, and because of their aloofness from society and concentration upon the closed circle of the family, they were invariably suspected of working for the destruction of all social structures.
> (Arendt, 1979, p 28)

The thesis that at one time some Jews exercised a useful function which offered them wealth and power, and that at some later point they lost power but retained their wealth, was clearly meant to apply unequally to Jews. The great Jewish financiers, for example, had been a tiny minority.

This leads directly onto the sixth point: Arendt's criticism of theories of antisemitism which treat it as an extreme form of ethnic nationalism. She argued that the rise of modern, political antisemitism was in an inverse relationship to the decline of nationalism and the nation state. 'The fact is', she wrote, that 'modern antisemitism grew in proportion as traditional nationalism declined and reached its climax at the exact moment when the European system of nation states and its precarious balance of power crashed' (1979, p 3). The Jews were resented as representatives of the nation state by those who came to be excluded from it.

Seventh, Arendt was critical of theories of antisemitism, like those to be found within a Marxist canon, whose focus on class relations and capitalist dynamics leaves no space for an understanding of the centrality of antisemitism in the development of modern politics.

> Twentieth-century political developments have driven the Jewish people into the storm centre of events; the Jewish Question and antisemitism, relatively unimportant phenomena in terms of world politics, became the catalytic agent first for the rise of the Nazi movement and the establishment of the organisational structure of the Third Reich, in which every citizen had to prove that he was not a Jew, then for a world war of unparalleled ferocity, and finally the emergence of the unprecedented crime of genocide in the midst of Occidental civilisation.
> (Arendt, 1979, p 3)

However, and this is the eighth point, Arendt was also critical of theories of antisemitism which divorce the phenomenon from 'wider' issues of the development of imperialism and totalitarianism. In its modern political form, antisemitism becomes increasingly separated from any internal history of Jewish–Gentile relations, and its ideological function increasingly loses contact with any reality.

> The emergence of the first antisemitic parties in the 1870s and 1880s marks the moment when the limited, factual basis of interest conflict and demonstrable experience was transcended, and that road opened which ended in the 'final solution'. From then on, in the era of imperialism, followed by the period of totalitarian movements and governments, it is no longer possible to isolate the Jewish question or the antisemitic ideology from issues that are actually almost completely unrelated to the realities of modern Jewish history. And this is not merely and not primarily because these matters played such a prominent role in world affairs, but because antisemitism was now being used for ulterior purposes that, though their implementation finally claimed Jews as their chief victims, left all particular issues of both Jewish and anti-Jewish interest far behind.
> (Arendt, 1979, p *xvi*)

Ninth, Arendt was critical of theories which reify the idea of 'the Jews' as if this corresponded unproblematically to an empirically verifiable and distinguishable group of people. Whether conceived religiously, culturally or ethnically, she argued that the same historical processes which gave birth to modern antisemitism also disaggregated the unity of Jews. The category of the Jews was certainly not simply the product of modern antisemitism (as it sometimes seemed to be presented in the writing of Jean-Paul Sartre)[1] but modern antisemitism reconstituted 'the Jews' as a unitary category precisely at the point when the process of dissolution of Jews into citizens was gathering pace. If the concept of 'the Jews' was not created by the antisemitic imagination, it was certainly fostered by it.

---

1 See Chapter 2 above.

Tenth, and lastly, Arendt argued that:

> nearly all elements [of antisemitism] that later crystallised in the novel totalitarian phenomenon ... had hardly been noticed by either learned or public opinion because they belonged to a subterranean stream of European history where, hidden from the light of the public and the attention of enlightened men, they had been able to gather an entirely unexpected virulence.
>
> (Arendt, 1979, p *xv*)

In other words, it was because antisemitism was largely hidden from history, except for a few 'non-Jewish crackpots and Jewish apologetics' (1979, p *xv*), that its virulence was so unexpected.

This reference to 'a subterranean stream ... hidden from the light' indicates why the choice has been made to explicate Arendt's thinking on antisemitism as a *genealogy*. It is a genealogy, first, because it investigates one incident or event and identifies several distinct strands or elements of that incident that can be pulled apart. When combined, they produce the outcome which is the subject of investigation. In the present case, that event is the 'Dreyfus Affair' and the following eruption of antisemitism that occurred in France at the turn of the twentieth century. Arendt's approach can be described as a genealogy because it uncovers those distinct strands that were previously hidden from history.

The elements that Arendt identifies in the Dreyfus Affair are, in fact, the political and social principles that were believed to bring into the world freedom and security. Consequently, concepts such as 'emancipation', 'equality' and 'rights' are interrogated so as to bring to light their meaning within the modern phenomenon of antisemitism. Arendt understands antisemitism as arising from within the framework of modernity itself, as the consequence of the 'normal functioning' of these Enlightenment and liberal principles. However, unlike those before her – such as Nietzsche,[2] who offers a radical critique of morality, finally calling for its overcoming – Arendt adopts a far more measured and ambivalent stance to these principles. In this way, Arendt differs from many of those who came after her, such as Bauman[3] who understands antisemitism as *inherent* in those principles. Rather, Arendt identifies *tendencies* in these principles whose negativity could only emerge when put into play through the praxis of historically located actors. The potentiality that is implicit within Arendt's genealogical method is reflected in her insistence that the outcome as to whether freedom or barbarity would prevail could be stated *a priori*.

---

2 See Chapters 4 and 5 above.
3 See Chapter 2 above.

The event that formed a centre-point for Arendt's investigation into antisemitism was the Dreyfus Affair that took place in France at the turn of the nineteenth century. She saw it as a 'kind of dress rehearsal for the performance of our own time' (1979, p 10) which demonstrated the 'hidden potentialities of antisemitism as a major political weapon within the framework of nineteenth century politics' (1979, p 10). It was around the common denominator of antisemitism, expressed in the street cry of 'Death to the Jews', that an otherwise disparate collection of groups – the Catholic clergy, the army, the aristocracy, the haute-bourgeoisie, the mob and the déclassé – could cohere. The unholy alliance contained those ruined by financial scandals of the late nineteenth century: the déclassé middle classes whose investments in government schemes had collapsed in a welter of incompetence, lies and bribery. The fact that Jews played only an insignificant role did not rob them of the illusion that they were to blame and that the Jews were the real power 'behind the throne'. It also contained those who never accepted the legitimacy of the new nation state and the principles of political equality on which it rested. Included under this category were the clergy, army officers and aristocracy whose animosity to Jews was fuelled not only by their gaining of political equality but also by their presence in the world of 'society'. It was this aspect of 'the Affair' that was expressed in the idea of 'Jewishness' as a racial characteristic that could be overcome neither by political equality nor by social assimilation. Finally, there were the bourgeoisie themselves who, although not driven by any direct conflict with Jews, were happy to see the blame for financial scandals placed upon the Jews and unwilling to act in their defence.

Arendt therefore sees the Dreyfus Affair as representing a coming together of political and social factors. She sees the Jews' political emancipation as complicated. The Jews' developing relationship with the nation state at the end of the nineteenth century appeared to be one marked by equality, but a combination of political factors ensured that that appearance was all it was. Additionally, although the political element determined the emergence of antisemitism, Arendt maintains that it is the social element, and its relationship to the political, that creates antisemitism's genocidal tendencies.

Beneath the superficial appearance that Jews were now equal rights-bearing persons, Arendt argues that civil and political rights were granted to Jews only inasmuch as they were Jews and performed specific services – mainly in the form of providing much needed financial resources – to the states which granted them these rights. At one level this continued an old tradition in which every Royal House would have its own 'Court Jew', but with the development of modern state machinery, the size of financial support was vastly increased and the 'state-Jews', as Arendt called them, could only find the quantities needed through organising the Jewish masses under their leadership. Consequently, both the states in question and their Jewish financiers were wary of complete Jewish emancipation for fear that, as a body, they would simply dissolve into the classes of civil society. The Jewish financiers demanded, and the states offered, equality as a reward for services rendered; on the other hand, both states and financiers sought to retain a distinct set of Jewish 'privileges'. Arendt argued that it was from this early history of bourgeois society that antisemitic images of the Jews were drawn: the identification of Jews with the state, the Jews as the secret power behind the throne, the Jews as a unitary and self-regarding entity outside of the nation, the Jews as a group that was privileged over the rest of the population, and the state as acting on behalf of Jewish interests. Since the large Jewish financial houses, like the House of Rothschild, had offices in many different countries, it also gave rise to the idea that the Jews were an international force, manipulating nation states to their own purposes. The notion of a 'Jewish World Conspiracy', most famously expressed in the Protocols of the Elders of Zion, emerged out of the role of Jews serving as channels of communication and peacebrokers in times of international conflict. These images, which represented a negative and selective reading of the real history of the Jews in early bourgeois society, took on a force of their own when, toward the end of the nineteenth century, the rise of imperialism made the function of Jews redundant and Jews became perceived as traitors and enemy agents.

Thus, with the defeat of Prussia by the French in 1807 and the ensuing period of reform, the Prussian aristocracy, resenting its loss of political power and prestige, began to argue that the state was now in Jewish hands. When the period of reaction began after 1815, liberals and radicals often turned anti-Jewish, claiming that under the new regime privileges were being granted to the Jews. In the 1870s and 1880s, when many of the middle classes lost their savings in a series of financial scandals, they pointed to the culpability of Jews as international bankers and financiers without commitment to any nation other than their own. The irony of this last period was that, at a time when the Jews were losing their position as state financiers and as international mediators, they were finally being granted full political rights. De Tocqueville's general rule, that a privileged man is best kicked when he is down, seemed to be validated.

Arendt first introduced the relationship between political and social factors through the 'garret' of Rahel Varnhagen at the turn of the eighteenth century. At a time when Jews suffered stringent legal and political disabilities, the world of 'society' was described by Arendt in terms of 'almost unbounded communication and intimacy' between individuals regardless of religion or rank (1979, p 60). However, when German Jews began (albeit unevenly) to be granted political emancipation under the post-Napoleonic reforming bureaucracy, 'society' began to ditch its Jewish contacts and relocate itself in the homes of the now disenfranchised aristocracy and higher echelons of the army. From this time on, Arendt argued, social relations between Jews and Gentiles never recovered their innocence.

With the early idyll of a mixed society, something disappeared which was never, in any country and at any other time, to return. Never again did any social group accept Jews with a free mind and heart. It would be friendly with Jews either because it was excited at its own daring and 'wickedness' or as a protest against making pariahs of fellow citizens.[4] But, wherever the Jews had ceased to be political and civil outcasts, they became social pariahs.

Arendt argued that the early idyll of a mixed society was from the start illusory and was, in fact, premised upon the concept of the 'exceptional Jews', especially those who had distinguished themselves from their co-religionists in the field of education, who were Jewish but at the same time different from the others. The 'exceptional Jew' expressed for Arendt an unhealthy mixture of attraction and repulsion that 'society' felt toward Jews, as well as the cost to Jews themselves (like Rahel Varnhagen) who were allowed to play the role of the parvenu only at the expense of breaking with the people of their birth. Arendt's story of Rahel Varnhagen[5] concerned the unhappiness of a parvenu life in which she was never allowed to forget her Jewish birth and was tortured by the memory of it. She lived in a kind of 'no-man's land' where she was both separated from 'her own people' and never secure within her adopted setting.

It was only when Jews were granted political emancipation, Arendt argued, that all strata of society began no longer to see exceptional Jews but the Jews as a group of whom the state was ready to make an exception. It was still easy for educated Jews to be distinguished and to distinguish themselves from the Jewish masses, but it became more difficult once Jews who wished to be admitted into non-Jewish society had to stand out against the phantom of 'the Jew'.

> No longer would it suffice to distinguish oneself from a more or less unknown mass of 'backward brethren'; one had to stand out – as an individual who could be congratulated on being an exception – from 'the Jew', and thus from the people as a whole.
> (Arendt, 1979, p 61)

Arendt saw in this social process the beginnings of the 'Jewish type' as an assemblage of 'psychological traits' said to constitute 'Jewishness'.

> The behaviour patterns of assimilated Jews, determined by this continuous concentrated effort to distinguish themselves, created a Jewish type that is recognisable everywhere. Instead of being defined by nationality or religion, Jews were being transformed into a social group whose members shared certain psychological attributes and reactions, the sum total

---

4 For a more extended discussion on this point, see Chapter 4 above.
5 See Arendt, 1997.

> of which constituted 'Jewishness'. In other words, Judaism became a psychological quality and the Jewish Question an involved personal problem for every individual Jew.
>
> (Arendt, 1979, p 66)

The idea that 'being Jewish' is an innate essence first came to light when the educated Jew was forced to live in the space 'between pariah and parvenu' and come to terms with his 'homelessness' from both Gentile and Jewish society.

> The majority of assimilated Jews thus lived in twilight of favour and misfortune and knew with certainty only that both success and failure were inextricably linked with the fact that they were Jews.
>
> (Arendt, 1979, p 66)

It was a difficult balance and the Jew had to present himself both as Jew and non-Jew. It was a balance that was important to maintain, however, because 'it was precisely this ambiguity of situation and character that made the relationship with the Jews attractive' (1979, p 66). The Jews themselves fostered the myth of being 'strange and exciting', as if their Jewishness really did exist and was worthy of universal interest.

The concept of 'Jewishness' as a racial characteristic, however, only became an integral part of antisemitic ideology at a time when Jewish emancipation into a disintegrating political world was occurring. At this time, the dialectic of attraction and repulsion toward Jews continued, for the doors of society could not resist accepting Jews on the basis of their 'secret vice', and the more Jews were threatened politically, the more society became interested in them. It seems that society's ambiguous attitude to the Jews could be satisfied only when they were held responsible for some large-scale crime, such as the alleged betrayal committed by Dreyfus, who appeared interesting until he was found not to be guilty. Then he could be quickly dropped. The section of Gentile society that was most interested in these newcomers was the bourgeoisie, whose lack of concern with political issues and feelings of boredom and ennui could be remedied by the presence of Jews.

When one Jew's guilt (as in the case of Dreyfus) could be attributed to all others, the concept of 'Jewishness' had arrived. The idea of 'guilt' was itself transformed into 'vice' – that is, 'from an act of will into an inherent, psychological quality which man cannot choose or reject but which is imposed upon him from without and which rules him as compulsively as the drug rules the addict' (1979, p 68). If in the past 'Jews had been able to escape from Judaism into conversion, from Jewishness there was no escape. A crime is met with punishment [but] a vice can only be exterminated' (1979, p 81).

Jews themselves played a part in this process.

> If it is true that 'Jewishness' could not have been perverted into an interesting vice without a prejudice which considered it a crime, it is also true that such perversion was made possible by those Jews who considered it an innate virtue.
>
> (Arendt, 1979, p 83)

On the one hand, the parvenu plays up his 'Jewishness' so as to gain social acceptance; on the other, beneath the apparent tolerance of Jews, society did not lose its instinct for hierarchy. The more equality was realised as a principle of political life, the more secretly was society rendered hierarchical (1979, p 86). The more threatened the Jews were politically, the more ambiguous was the philosemitism which 'ends always by adding to political antisemitism that mysterious fanaticism without which antisemitism could hardly have become the best slogan for organising the masses' (1979, p 86). Moreover, a genocidal instinct born of social resentment is multiplied by what Arendt calls a 'psychological truth in the scapegoat theory' (1979, p 8). If and when antisemitic episodes actually lead to antisemitic legislation (as in Germany), the society that had 'accepted' Jews will seek to purge themselves 'of a secret viciousness, to cleanse themselves of a stigma which they had mysteriously and wickedly loved' (1979, p 86).

Arendt brought to the surface the origins of antisemitism in the political and social history of Jewish emancipation. Her genealogy of antisemitism referred to that which was 'unaccounted for in political history, hidden under the surface of events' (1979, p *xv*). A purely political history of the causes of antisemitism might have explained anti-Jewish legislation or even mass expulsion, but hardly wholesale extermination. Modern antisemitic ideology came to the fore when the nation state, the bulwark of the old political order, was in the throes of disintegration and an ever-increasing number of people were excluded from the structures of the state and civil society.[6] That these elements should crystallise around antisemitism was explained not only as the consequence of the fact that the Jews appeared to represent that political body, but also by the fact that, when emancipation and assimilation were finally granted, they were based on entry into an increasingly antisemitic and hostile world. Stripped of any useful function as possessors of wealth without power, the Jews were more exposed to danger than before. It was at this moment that antisemitism lost almost any connection with the reality of the world.

Devoid of any contact with the empirical world, antisemitism crystallised into an ideology and became one element amongst others in the new totalitarian world, of which the mass killings of the Third Reich was a part. Whilst this later development is beyond the scope of the current study, one aspect of the 'final catastrophe' is of relevance in the present context. Why, Arendt

---

6 See Chapter 6 above.

asks, did the institution of rights fail to protect the Jews and others once antisemitism had become an 'origin of totalitarianism'? Why, when those outcast from their body politic had nothing else to rely upon, did they appear to crumble as so many pieces of paper?

In the section of the *Origins* entitled 'The Perplexities of the Rights of Man', Arendt discusses this problem in detail. Her thesis is that from their inception, human rights, as encapsulated within the 'Rights of Man', had always been inescapably bound up with the 'right of the people to sovereign self-government'.

> Man had hardly appeared as a completely emancipated isolated being who carried his dignity within himself without reference to some larger encompassing order, when he disappeared again into a member of a people. From the beginning the paradox involved in the declaration of inalienable human rights was that it was reckoned with an 'abstract' human being who seemed to exist nowhere, for even savages lived in some kind of a social order.
>
> (Arendt, 1979, p 291)

However, this paradox only fully came to light at precisely the moment that people appeared in the world whose only claim to protection rested precisely on these 'abstract' human rights. Thus, as Arendt observes, even before one could claim his or her human rights, one first needed to possess a 'right to have rights' – a 'right to belong to some kind of organised community' (1979, pp 296–7). Yet, it was exactly this fundamental, prior and hitherto invisible '*grundnorm*' that those cast out from their place of residence were lacking. Without membership of a sovereign state, therefore, human rights, hitherto believed to be 'inalienable', were unenforceable and, to all intents and purposes, meaningless.

Arendt argues that it was not so much the dispossessed exclusion from one body politic that was to prove fatal to so many, but rather that no space remained in the world that was not incorporated within the system of nations.

> Nobody had been aware that mankind, for so long a time considered under the image of a family of nations, had reached the stage where whoever was thrown out of these tightly organised closed communities found himself thrown out of the family of nations altogether.
>
> (Arendt, 1979, p 294)

That the loss of membership from one's own national community led to such complete exclusion arose also from the fact that, within this tightly knit family, each body politic was connected with others through various international treaties, the consequence of which was that a person's legal status, provided by their initial citizenship, travelled with the person themselves. As such, 'whoever is no longer caught [in the web spun by this organisation of nations] finds himself out of legality altogether' (1979, p 294). From that moment on, in a world where 'the loss of polity itself expels [a person] from humanity' (1979, p 297), one's continued existence, one's life, is no longer guaranteed, but depends either on the kindness and charity of others, or is ended by those who had ensured that the verdict of 'superfluousness' they had passed on these people was shared with others. In this way,

> because the incredible plight of an ever-growing group of innocent people was like a practical demonstration of the totalitarian movements' cynical claims that no such thing as inalienable rights existed and that the affirmations of the democracies to the contrary were mere prejudice, hypocrisy, and cowardice in the face of the cruel majesty of a new world. The very phrase 'human rights' became for all concerned – victims, persecutors, and onlookers alike – the evidence of hopeless idealism or fumbling feeble-minded hypocrisy.
>
> (Arendt, 1979, p 269)

Despite her critique of the limitations of human rights, Arendt maintains that they are still of significance for the development of a civilised world. Following Aristotle, Arendt characterises a truly *human* life as one spent within a political community, a sphere in which rights and equality are both desirable and necessary. Indeed, she notes that the first step the Nazis took on their way to extermination was to deprive Jews of their political and civil rights. Thus, Arendt notes the correspondence between the denial of rights and the loss of civilisation.

Arendt's critique of rights must be read in the context of the development that arose as a consequence of imperialism whereby the nation subsumed the function of the state, and in which the universality of rights was replaced with the particularity of ethnicity as the mark of membership. Correspondingly, Arendt makes a distinction between the realm of public life and the realm of private life. Whilst in public (that is, political) life, relations between citizens should be governed by the principles of equality, justice and rights, within the realm of private life, in which individuals' innate uniqueness cannot and should not be suppressed, these political principles are inapplicable. Instead, relations in private life,

> can adequately be dealt with only by the unpredictable hazards of friendship and sympathy, or by the great and incalculable grace of love, which says with Augustine, '*Volo ut sis* (I want you to be)', without being

able to give any particular reason for such supreme and unsurpassable affirmation.

(Arendt, 1979, p 301)[7]

Arendt argues, however, that the equality of the political realm, in contradistinction to the naturalness that should prevail in the private realm, is itself a product of the human artifice, of the act of human labour in and through the 'build[ing] of a common world' (1979, p 301) which can only be accomplished by those recognised as equals.

However, such a construction of equality at the level of the private realm is not only misplaced but threatens to eradicate the natural uniqueness which inheres in each and every individual and which can only thrive outside such principles of equality and universal rights. Nonetheless, Arendt argues that it is precisely this naturalness that comes to represent the greatest fear to the hubris of a humanity who increasingly comes to believe that nothing is itself beyond its own powers.

> The more highly developed a civilisation, the more accomplished the world it has produced, the more at home men feel within the human artifice – the more they will resent everything they have not produced, everything that is merely and mysteriously given them.
>
> (Arendt, 1979, pp 300–1)

Thus, to reduce the fear that innate difference produces in the realm of the 'human artifice', the modern body politic will insist on the 'ethnic homogeneity' of their population. Within this context, those who are – or, rather, are said to be – different will come to represent the limits of human activity and act as a provocation to the alleged omnipotence of 'civilised man', who will treat that incitement with a 'distinct tendency to destroy' (1979, p 301).[8]

This fear and resentment of the 'alien' of the different and the unique (that is, natural) – which, in an increasingly nationally (that is, ethnically) divided world can only produce increasing violence – is further fuelled by the appearance of large numbers of rightless individuals. Those deprived of the right to have rights, unable to claim any affiliation to a body politic, will be left with nothing other than their basic 'humanness'. In this situation, such an expression refers to nothing more than a claim to the 'minimum fact of their human origin' and, as such, have only the 'right of the naked savage' (1979, p 300).[9]

---

7 For an intricate and interesting discussion of Arendt's relationship to the thought of Augustine, see Arendt, 1996.
8 The theme of civilisation and naturalness is developed and radicalised in the thought of Adorno and Horkheimer, Zygmunt Bauman and Giorgio Agamben; see Chapter 2 above.
9 Thomas Payne's introduction to Edward Burke's *Reflections on the Revolution in France*, 1790 (quoted in Arendt, 1979).

Deprived of a truly human (that is, political) existence, these 'savages' are thrown back into a 'peculiar state of nature', where their only attributes are the unique and natural attributes granted them through the accident of their births. Thus, from the perspective of those in whose midst they find themselves, they come to embody the difference of nature thought to have been finally defeated. As such, they will call down upon themselves the resentful violence of those threatened by such an appearance.

And it is at this point that Arendt notes the emergence of a modern vicious circle. The more civilisation produces savages, the more it produces barbarians who, in turn, produce more savages and so on. As she states,

> [t]he danger is that a global, universally interrelated civilisation may produce barbarians from its own midst by forcing millions of people into conditions which, despite all appearance, are the conditions of savages.
> (Arendt, 1979, p 302)

As an historical explanation, Arendt's was, of course, incomplete. Thus the Jews of whom Arendt wrote were confined to a small section of the Jewish 'community' as a whole: its financial and intellectual elite. They were the ones living between 'pariah and parvenu', the space which gave rise to a specific 'Jewish type' that was to have such devastating consequences. The inference could be made that here this 'type' was in fact a product of embryonic antisemitism. To a great degree this is correct. However, it is also the case that in keeping with her determination to allocate to Jews their role of responsibility in the events that drove them into the 'storm centre of events', she stresses that at all times a choice remained open as to whether to 'play the role' or not. As she states,

> [i]f it is true that 'Jewishness' could not have been perverted into an interesting vice without a prejudice which considered it a crime, it is also true that such perversion was made possible by those Jews who considered it an innate virtue.
> (Arendt, 1979, p 83)

The vast majority of Jews, whom Arendt termed the 'Jewish masses', were subsumed under the hegemony of their leaders. She recognised that the modern Jewish communities were as stratified as everyone else, but the actions and agency of the Jewish masses are given no independent role in the analysis. For an analysis of these class relations, we have to look elsewhere.

As an understanding of the roots of antisemitism, the question Arendt addresses is how antisemitism, which was a relatively unimportant phenomenon in terms of world politics, came to play such a central role in the history of Europe. She distinguishes between pre-modern forms of anti-Jewish animosity and modern antisemitism without ignoring the modern uses of explanations of pre-modern prejudices against the Jews. The configuration of elements to create the Jews, antisemites and antisemitism are all explained through a focus that never reaches beyond modernity. Consequently, unlike, for example, Nietzsche, Sartre and Bauman, Arendt has no need to explain modern antisemitism through recourse to a pre-existing prejudice against the Jews. Rather, she highlights[10] the distinction between pre-modern forms of anti-Jewish animosity and modern antisemitism and its conditions of existence.

Arendt neither falls back into the idea that antisemitism represents a harking back to the past or a reaction against modernity; nor conversely does she propose that antisemitism is the logical product of modernity itself. In her analysis, antisemitism does not represent the futility of political emancipation or the rights of man, still less their alleged collaboration with genocide. Her account of the inability of human rights to protect those sent to their slaughter serves not as a call for their negation, but as a critical summons to strengthen them and their enforcement, along with a truly human (that is, political) equality, in which one's uniqueness is also permitted its expression.

---

10 It is, of course, true that her starting point refers back to the pre-nation state 'Court Jews', but even here they are clearly distinguishable from the later 'State Jews'.

Bibliography

Abrahams, I, *Jewish Life in the Middle Ages*, 1969, Philadelphia: JPS
Adorno, TW, *Negative Dialectics*, Ashton, B (trans), 1973, London: Routledge
Adorno, TW, *Mimina Moralia*, 1978, London: Verso
Adorno, TW, *Negative Dialectics*, 1990, London: Routledge
Adorno, TW, 'The stars down to earth', in *The Stars Down to Earth and Other Essays on the Irrational in Culture*, 1994a, London: Routledge
Adorno, TW, 'Theses against occultism', in *The Stars Down to Earth and Other Essays on the Irrational in Culture*, 1994b, London: Routledge
Adorno, TW, 'Research project on anti-semitism', in *The Stars Down to Earth and Other Essays on the Irrational in Culture*, 1994c, London: Routledge
Adorno, TW, 'Anti-semitism and fascist propaganda', in *The Stars Down to Earth and Other Essays on the Irrational in Culture*, 1994d, London: Routledge
Adorno, TW and Horkheimer, M, *Dialectic of Enlightenment*, Jephcott, E (trans), Noerr, GS (ed), 2002, Stanford: Stanford University Press
Agamben, G, *Homo Sacer: Sovereign Power and Bare Life*, 1995, Stanford: Stanford University Press
Agamben, G, *Remnants of Auschwitz: the Witness and the Archive*, 2002, New York: Zone Books
Agamben, G, *State of Exception*, 2004, Chicago: Chicago University Press
Ansell-Pearson, K, *An Introduction to Nietzsche as Political Thinker*, 1994, Cambridge: Cambridge University Press
Anthias, F and Yuval-Davis, N, *Racialized Boundaries*, 1993, London: Routledge
Arato, A and Gebhart, E, *The Essential Frankfurt School Reader*, 1995, New York: Continuum
Arendt, H, *Eichmann in Jerusalem: a Report on the Banality of Evil*, 1964, New York: Viking Press
Arendt, H, *On Violence*, 1970, Orlando: Harcourt, Brace and Co
Arendt, H, *Origins of Totalitarianism*, 1979, London: Harcourt, Brace and Co
Arendt, H, *The Human Condition*, 1989, London: University of Chicago Press
Arendt, H, *On Revolution*, 1990, London: Penguin
Arendt, H, *Essays in Understanding*, 1994, New York: Schocken
Arendt, H, *Love and Saint Augustine*, 1996, London: University of Chicago Press
Arendt, H, *Rahel Varnhagen*, 1997, Baltimore: The John Hopkins University Press
Avineri, S, *The Social and Political Thought of Karl Marx*, 1968, Cambridge: Cambridge University Press

Bauer, B, *The Jewish Question*, 1843a, Brunswick
Bauer, B, 'The capacity of present-day Jews and Christians to become free', in *Einundzwanzig Bogen aus der Schweiz*, 1843b, Zurich: Verlag des Literarischen Comptoirs
Bauman, Z, *Legislators and Interpreters*, 1987, Oxford: Polity Press
Bauman, Z, *Modernity and the Holocaust*, 1991, Oxford: Polity Press
Bauman, Z, *Modernity and Ambivalence*, 1993a, Oxford: Polity Press
Bauman, Z, *Postmodern Ethics*, 1993b, Oxford: Blackwell
Benhabib, S, *The Reluctant Modernism of Hannah Arendt*, 1996, London: Sage
Benjamin, A (ed), *The Lyotard Reader*, 1989, Oxford: Blackwell
Benjamin, A, *Judging Lyotard*, 1992, London: Routledge
Benjamin, W, *The Origin of German Tragic Drama*, 2003, London, Verso
Bernstein, MA, *Foregone Conclusions: Against Apocalyptic History*, 1994, London: University of California Press
Bernstein, R, *Hannah Arendt and the Jewish Question*, 1996, Cambridge: Polity
Bettlelheim, B, *Recollections and Reflections*, 1990, London: Thames and Hudson
Bittler, R, '*Ressentiment*' in Schacht, R, *Nietzsche, Genealogy, Morality: Essays on Nietzsche's* On the Genealogy of Morals, 1994, London, University of California Press
Blondel, E, 'The question of genealogy', in Schacht, R, *Nietzsche, Genealogy, Morality: Essays on Nietzsche's* On the Genealogy of Morals, 1994, London, University of California Press
Brinker, M, 'Nietzsche and the Jews', in Golomb, J and Wistrich, R (eds), *Nietzsche, Godfather of Fascism: on the Uses and Abuses of a Philosophy*, 2002, Oxford: Princeton University Press
Browning, C, *The Path to Genocide: Essays on Launching the Final Solution*, 1992, Cambridge: Cambridge University Press
Carlbach, J, *Karl Marx and the Radical Critique of Judaism*, 1978, London: Routledge and Kegan Paul
Cohen, S, *That's Funny, You Don't Look Anti-Semitic*, 1984, Leeds: Beyond the Pale Collective
Cohn, N, *Warrant for Genocide*, 1967, London: Eyre and Spottiswoode
Conway, DW, 'Genealogy and critical method', in Schacht, R, *Nietzsche, Genealogy, Morality: Essays on Nietzsche's* On the Genealogy of Morals, 1994, London: University of California Press
Conway, DW, *Nietzsche and the Political*, 1997, London: Routledge
Cotterrell, R, *The Politics of Jurisprudence: a Critical Introduction to Legal Philosophy*, 2nd edn, 2003, London: Lexis Nexis
Deleuze, G, *Nietzsche and Philosophy*, Tomlinson, H (trans), 1983, London: Athlone Press
Diduck, A and Kaganas, F, *Family Law, Gender and the State*, 1999, Oxford: Hart
Dimont, MI, *The Indestructible Jews*, 1971, Toronto: Signet
Draper, H, *Karl Marx's Theory of Revolution, State and Bureaucracy*, 1977, New York: Monthly Review Press
Duffy, MF and Mittleman, W, 'Nietzsche's attitude toward the Jews', (1988) *Journal of the History of Ideas* 49(2): 301–17
Edwards, J, *The Jews in Western Europe 1400–1600*, 1994, Manchester: Manchester University Press
Fine, R, *Political Investigations: Hegel, Marx, Arendt*, 2001, London: Routledge

Fine, R and Hirsh, D, 'The decision to commit a crime against humanity', in Archer, M and Tritter, J (eds), *Rational Choice Theory: Resisting Colonization*, 2002, London: Routledge

Fitzpatrick, P, 'Bare sovereignty: *Homo Sacer* and the insistence of law', in Norris, A (ed), *Politics, Metaphysics and Death: Essays on Giorgio Agamben's* Homo Sacer, 2005, London: Duke University

Foucault, M, *Society Must Be Defended*, 2001, London: Penguin

Foucault, M, 'Nietzsche, genealogy, history', in Richardson, J (ed), *Nietzsche*, 2001, Oxford: Oxford University Press

Freeman, M, (ed), *Lloyd's Introduction to Jurisprudence* 7th edn, 2001, London: Sweet and Maxwell

Freud, S, *On Metapsychology*, 1991, London: Penguin

Freud, S, *Civilisation, Society and Religion*, 1991a, London: Penguin

Freud, S, *The Origins of Religion*, 1991b, London: Penguin

Georges, J and Ghaleigh, NS, *Darker Legacies of Law in Europe: the Shadow of National Socialism and Fascism over Europe and its Legal Tradition*, 2003, Oxford: Oxford University Press

Gerth, HH and Wright Mills, C (eds), *From Max Weber*, 1970, London: Routledge and Kegan Paul

Gilman, SL and Katz, ST (eds), *Anti-Semitism in Times of Crisis*, 1991, New York: NYU Press

Goldhagen, D, *Hitler's Willing Executioners: Ordinary Germans and the Holocaust*, 1996, London: Little, Brown and Co.

Golomb, J (ed), *Nietzsche and Jewish Culture*, 1997, London: Routledge

Golomb J and Wistrich, R (eds), *Nietzsche, Godfather of Fascism: on the Uses and Abuses of a Philosophy*, 2002, Oxford: Princeton University Press

Goodrich, P, 'Law in the courts of love: Andreas Capellus and the judgment of love', (1996) 48 *Stanford Law Review* 160

Halevi, I, *A History of the Jews: Ancient and Modern*, 1987, London: Zed Books

Hartman, G, *The Longest Shadow: in the Aftermath of the Holocaust*, 1996, Basingstoke: Palgrave Macmillan

Hartman, G, *Scars of the Spirit: the Struggle against Inauthenticity*, 2002, New York: Palgrave Macmillan

Hegel, GWF, *The Philosophy of History*, Sibree, J (trans), 1956, Toronto: Dover

Hegel, GWF, *The Phenomenology of Mind*, Baillie, JB (trans), 1967, New York: Harper Torchbooks

Hegel, GWF, *Natural Law*, Knox, TM (trans), 1975, Philadelphia: University of Pennsylvania Press

Hegel, GWF, *Faith and Knowledge*, Cerf, W and Harris, HS (trans), 1977, New York: State University of New York Press

Hegel, GWF, *Elements of the Philosophy of Right*, Nisbet, HB (trans), 1991, Cambridge: Cambridge University Press

Hilberg, R, *Perpetrators, Victims, Bystanders: the Jewish Catastrophe 1933–1945*, 1993, London: Lime Tree

Jacobson, AJ and Schlink, B (eds), *Weimar: a Jurisprudence of Crisis*, 2002, Berkeley: University of California Press

Jameson, F, *Late Marxism: Adorno or the Persistence of the Dialectic*, 1990, London: Verso

Jarvis, S, *Adorno: a Critical Introduction*, 1998, Oxford: Polity Press
Jaskot, PB, *The Architecture of Oppression: the SS, Forced Labour and the Nazi Monumental Building Economy*, 2000, London: Routledge
Kalyvas, A, 'The sovereign weaver: beyond the camp', in Norris, A (ed), *Politics, Metaphysics and Death: Essays on Giorgio Agamben's* Homo Sacer, 2005, London: Duke University
Kalmar, I, *The Trotskys, Freuds and Woody Allens: Portrait of a Culture*, 1994, London: Penguin
Kant, I, *Critique of Pure Reason*, 1934, London: Everyman Press
Kant, I, *Critique of Practical Reason*, Beck, LW (trans), 1958, Indianapolis: Bolts Merill
Kant, I, *The Metaphysics of Morals*, Gregor, M (trans), 1996, Cambridge: Cambridge University Press
Kant, I, *Critique of Judgement*, 2000, Cambridge: Cambridge University Press
Kaplan, GT and Kessler, CS (eds), *Hannah Arendt: Thinking, Judging Freedom*, 1989, London: Allen and Unwin
Katz, J, *From Prejudice to Destruction: Anti-Semitism 1700–1933*, 1980, Cambridge: Harvard
Klemperer, V, *The Klemperer Diaries*, Chalmers, M (trans), 1999, London: Phoenix
Koehler, J, *Nietzsche and Wagner: a Lesson in Subjugation*, Taylor, R (trans), 1998, London: Yale University Press
Korner, S, *Kant*, 1955, London: Penguin
Kritzman, LD, 'In the shadows of Auschwitz: culture, memories, and self-reflection', in Kritzman, LD (ed), *Auschwitz and After: Race, Culture, and 'the Jewish Question' in France*, 1995, London: Routledge
Leiter, B, *Nietzsche on Morality*, 2002, London: Routledge
Leon, A, *The Jewish Question*, 1970, London: Pathfinder Press
Levi, P, *If This is a Man*, 1987, London: Abacus
Levinas, E, *Ethics and Infinity: Conversations with Philippe Nemo*, Cohen, R (trans), 1982, Pittsburgh: Duquesne University Press
Levinas, E, *The Levinas Reader*, 1989, Oxford: Blackwell
Lindemann, AS, *The Jew Accused: Three Anti-Semitic Affairs (Dreyfus, Beilis, Frank) 1894–1915*, 1993, Cambridge: Cambridge University Press
Locke, J, *Two Treatises of Government*, 1998, Cambridge: Cambridge University Press
Lowith, K, *Max Weber and Karl Marx*, 1993, London: Routledge
Lyotard, J-F, *The Postmodern Condition: a Report on Knowledge*, 1984, Manchester: Manchester University Press
Lyotard, J-F, *The Differend: Phrases in Dispute*, 1988, Minnesota: University of Minnesota Press
Lyotard, J-F, *Heidegger and 'the jews'*, Michel, A and Roberts, M (trans), 1990, Minneapolis: University of Minnesota Press
Lyotard, J-F, 'The Grip (*Mainmise*)', in *Political Writings*, Readings, B and Geiman, KP (trans), 1993, London: UCL Press
Lyotard, J-F, 'German guilt', in *Political Writings*, Readings, B and Geiman, KP (trans), 1993, London: UCL Press
Lyotard J-F, '*Heidegger and "the jews"*: a conference in Vienna and Freiburg', in *Political Writings*, Readings, B and Geiman, KP (trans), 1993, London: UCL Press

Lyotard, J-F, 'Europe, the Jews, and the Book', in *Political Writings*, Readings, B and Geiman, KP (trans), 1993, London: UCL Press
Lyotard, J-F, *The Inhuman*, 1993, Cambridge: Polity Press
Lyotard, J-F, *Lessons on the Analytic of the Sublime*, Rottenberg, E (trans), 1994, Stanford: Stanford University Press
MacIntyre, A, 'Genealogies and subversion', in Schacht, R, *Nietzsche, Genealogy, Morality: Essays on Nietzsche's* On the Genealogy of Morals, 1994, London: University of California Press
MacMillan, J, 'Unholier than Thou, *Guardian Review*, 11 October 2003
Manderson, D, 'From hunger to love: myths of the source, interpretation, and constitution of law in children's literature', (2003) 15 *Law and Literature* 87
Mandle, S, 'Introduction', in Salome, L, *Nietzsche*, 2001, Chicago: University of Illinois Press
Marcuse, H, *Reason and Revolution*, 1986, London: RKP
Marrus, M, *The Holocaust in History*, 1989, London: Penguin
Marx, K, *The Poverty of Philosophy*, 1958, Moscow: Progress
Marx, K, *The Poverty of Philosophy*, 1978, Moscow: Progress
Marx, K, 'On the Jewish Question', in Colletti, L (ed), *Early Writings*, 1992, London: Penguin
Marx, K, 'A contribution to the critique of Hegel's Philosophy of Right, Introduction', in Colletti, L (ed), *Early Writings*, 1992, London: Penguin
Marx, K, 'Economic and philosophical manuscripts', in Colletti, L (ed), *Early Writings*, 1992, London: Penguin
Marx, K, 'Critical notes on the article "The King of Prussia and social reform by a Prussian" ' in Colletti, L (ed), *Early Writings*, 1992, London: Penguin
Marx, K, *Capital*, 1995, Oxford: Oxford University Press
Marx, K, 'The eighteenth Brumaire of Louis Bonaparte', in Carver, T (ed), *Later Political Writings*, 1996, Cambridge: Cambridge University Press
Marx, K, 'The Communist Manifesto', in Carver, T (ed), *Later Political Writings*, 1996, Cambridge: Cambridge University Press
Mesnard, P, 'The political philosophy of Giorgio Agamben: a critical evaluation', in *Totalitarian Movements and Political Religions*, Vol 5, No 1, Summer 2004, pp 139–57
Millington, B, *Wagner*, 2000, Oxford: Oxford University Press
Mills, C, 'Linguistic survival and ethicality: biopolitics, subjectivation, and testimony in *Remnants of Auschwitz*', in Norris, A (ed), *Politics, Metaphysics and Death: Essays on Giorgio Agamben's* Homo Sacer, 2005, London: Duke University
Mosse, GL, *Toward the Final Solution: A History of European Racism*, 1980, Toronto: Harper Colophone Books
Mosse, GL, *Confronting the Nation: Jewish and Western Nationalism*, 1993, New England: Brandeis
Najarian, J, 'Gnawing at history: the rhetoric of Holocaust denial', 39 *The Midwest Quarterly* 74
Nietzsche, FW, *Birth of Tragedy*, Kaufman, W (trans), 1967, London: Random House
Nietzsche, FW, *Untimely Mediations*, 1983, Cambridge: Cambridge University Press
Nietzsche, FW, *Ecce Homo*, Kaufmann, W (trans), 1989, New York: Vintage
Nietzsche, FW, *Beyond Good and Evil*, Hollingdale, RJ (trans), 1990, London: Penguin
Nietzsche, FW, *Human, All Too Human*, 1994, London: Penguin

Nietzsche, FW, *On the Genealogy of Morals*, Ansell-Pearson, K (ed), 2002, Cambridge: Cambridge University Press
Norris, A, 'Giorgio Agamben and the politics of the living dead', in Norris, A (ed), *Politics, Metaphysics and Death: Essays on Giorgio Agamben's* Homo Sacer, 2005, London: Duke University
Paddison, M, *Adorno's Aesthetics of Music*, 1993, Cambridge: Cambridge University Press
Postone, M and Santer, E, *Meaning and Catastrophe: the Holocaust and the Twentieth Century*, 2003, Chicago: Chicago University Press
Postone, M, *Anti-Semitism and National Socialism*, 2000, London: Chronos Publications
Pulzer, P, *Jews and the German State: the Political History of a Minority, 1848–1933*, 1992, Oxford: Blackwell
Rabinach, A, ' "Why were the Jews sacrificed?" The place of antisemitism in Adorno and Horkheimer's *Dialectic of Enlightenment*', in Gibson, N and Rubin, R (eds), *Adorno: A Critical Reader*, 2002, Oxford: Blackwell
Rennap, I, *Anti-Semitism and the Jewish Question*, 1942, London: Lawrence and Wishart
Richardson, J (ed), *Nietzsche*, 2001, Oxford: Oxford University Press
Rose, G, *The Melancholy Science: an Introduction to the Thought of Theodore W Adorno*, 1978, London: Macmillan
Rose, G, *Hegel Contra Sociology*, 1981, London: Athlone
Rose, G, *The Broken Middle*, 1992, Oxford: Blackwell
Rose, G, *Judaism and Modernity*, 1993, Oxford: Blackwell
Rose, G, *Mourning Becomes the Law: Philosophy and Representation*, 1996, Cambridge: Cambridge University Press
Rose, PL, *German Question/Jewish Question: Revolutionary Anti-Semitism from Kant to Wagner*, 1990, New Jersey: Princeton University Press
Rotenstreich, N, *Jews and German Philosophy*, 1984, New York: Schoken
Rousseau, E, *The Social Contract*, 1968, London: Penguin
Rybalka, M, 'Publication and reception of *Anti-Semite and Jew*', 87 October 161 (Winter 1999)
Safranski, R, *Nietzsche: a Philosophical Biography*, 2002, London: Granta
Sartre, JP, *Search for a Method*, 1968, New York: Vintage Books
Sartre, JP, *Anti-Semite and Jew*, 1995, New York: Schoken
Sartre, JP, 'Reflections on the Jewish Question – a lecture', 87 *October* 32 (Winter 1999)
Schache, W (1968) 'Nazi architecture and its approach to antiquity: a criticism of the Neoclassical Argument, with reference to the Berlin Museum Plans', 1968
Schacht, R, *Nietzsche, Genealogy, Morality: Essays on Nietzsche's* On the Genealogy of Morals, 1994, London: University of California Press
Scheler, M, *Ressentiment*, 2003, Milwaukee: Marquette University Press
Schrift, AD, *Nietzsche's French Legacy: a Genealogy of Poststructuralism*, 1995, London: Routledge
Schmitt, C, *The Crisis of Political Democracy*, Kennedy, E (trans), 1988, London: The MIT Press
Schmitt, C, *The Concept of the Political*, Schwab, G (trans), 1996, London: University of Chicago Press
Scobie, A, (1990) *Hitler's State Architecture: the Impact of Classical Antiquity*, 1990, Pennsylvania: Penn State Press

Sendak, M, *Where the Wild Things Are*, 1991, 2000, London: Red Fox
Seymour, DM, 'Letter from Shylock', (1997) 2 *Law and Critique* 215
Seymour, DM, 'Adorno and Horkheimer: Enlightenment and antisemitism', Oxford Journal of Jewish Studies, (2000) 51 *Journal of Jewish Studies* 297, and in *Theodore W. Adorno*, Delanty, G (ed), 2004, London: Sage
Seymour, DM, 'Lyotard: emancipation, antisemitism and "the Jews"', in Fine, R and Turner, C, *Social Theory after the Holocaust*, 2000, Liverpool: Liverpool University Press
Seymour, DM, 'Representation and the framing of modernity', (2001) 10 *Griffith Law Review* 259
Seymour, DM, 'Film and law: in search of a critical method', in Moran, L, Christie, I and Louzidou, E, *Law's Moving Image*, 2004, London: Glasshouse
Shakespeare, W, *The Merchant of Venice*, 1967, London: Penguin
Silk, MS and Stern, JP, *Nietzsche on Tragedy*, 1981, Cambridge: Cambridge University Press
Sim, S, *Jean-Francois Lyotard*, 1996, Hemel Hempstead: Prentice Hall / Harvester Wheatsheaf
Singer, P, *Hegel*, 1983, Oxford: Oxford University Press
Smith, A, *Wealth of Nations*, 1991, London: Everyman's Library
Spotts, F, *Hitler and the Power of Aesthetics*, 2002, London: Hutchinson
Stern, JP, *Nietzsche*, 1985, London: Fontana
Stone, A, 'Adorno and the disenchantment of nature', in (2006) *Philosophy and Social Criticism* 32:2
Stolleis, M, *The Law under the Swastika*, 1999, Chicago: Chicago University Press
Tenzo, E, 'The blindness of the intellectuals: historicizing Sartre's *Anti-Semite and Jew*', 87 *October* 73 (Winter 1999)
Till, N, *Mozart and the Enlightenment*, 1994, London: Faber and Faber
Traverso, E, *The Marxists and the Jewish Question: the History of a Debate (1843–1943)*, 1994, New York: Humanity Books
Twining, W, *Legal Theory and Common Law*, 1986, Oxford: Blackwell
van Pelt, RJ and Westfall, CW, *Architectural Principles in the Age of Historicism*, 1993, London: Yale University Press
Villa, D, *Politics, Philosophy, Terror: Essays on the Thoughts of Hannah Arendt*, 1999, Princeton, NJ: Princeton University Press
Weber, M, *The Protestant Ethic and the Spirit of Capitalism*, Parsons, T (trans), 1930, London: Harper Collins
Wicks, R, *Nietzsche*, 2002, Oxford: One World
Williams, WD, 'Nietzsche's masks', in *Nietzsche*, Pasley, M (ed), 1978, London: Methuen
Williams, J, *Lyotard: Towards a Postmodern Philosophy*, 1998, Oxford: Polity Press
Wood, AW, *Hegel's Ethical Thought*, 1990, Cambridge: Cambridge University Press
Yovel, Y, 'Nietzsche, the Jews, and *Ressentiment*', in *Nietzsche, Genealogy, Morality: Essays on Nietzsche's* On the Genealogy of Morals, Schact, R (ed), 1994, London: University of California Press
Yovel, Y, *Dark Riddle: Hegel, Nietzsche, and the Jews*, 1998, Pennsylvania: Pennsylvania State University Press
Yovel, Y, 'Nietzsche *contra* Wagner on the Jews', in Golomb, J and Wistrich, R (eds), *Nietzsche, Godfather of Fascism: on the Uses and Abuses of a Philosophy*, 2002, Oxford: Princeton University Press

Index

Page references to footnotes are followed by the letter 'n'. Titles of publications beginning with 'A' or 'The' are listed under the first significant word.

absence, critique of modernity upon 33
absolute, the 38–9
Adorno, Theodor W: on absolute 39; and Agamben 26; and Bauman 19–20, 23, 24; on causality 15, 16, 24, 30; on concentration camps 111; on contradiction 36; on Enlightenment 13, 14–18, 19–20, 26; on Holocaust 19, 33; imminent critique *see* immanent critique; and irony 84–5; on knowledge and domination 40; on Nazism 100; on positivism 41n; on social theory 110–11; on utopia 37–8
aestheticaton, and consumption 39–45, 47
Agamben, Giorgio 14, 26–31, 33, 49, 75–80; on biopolitics 27–31, 76, 78; on emancipation 75, 76, 78, 79, 81; on *Musselman* 77, 78, 79; on Nazism 29–30, 31, 77–8; *Remnants of Auschwitz* 27; on *ressentiment* 75, 76, 79, 80, 81; on Rights of Man/Rights of the Citizen 76
ancien regime 27, 76
Ancient Greeks 85, 94, *see also* Aristotle; Socrates
anti-capitalist antisemitism 8n
anti-emancipationist argument, Marx on 1–11
Anti-Semite and Jew (Sartre) 60, 67
antisemitism theories, criticism 113–16
Apollo 85, 103, 106
architecture: Hitler on 103–4; monumental *see* monumental architecture, Nazi

Arendt, Hannah xxi, 13, 23; antisemitism theories, criticism 113–16; on concentration camps 109; on Dreyfus Affair 116, 117; on emancipation and antisemitism 50; on 'exceptional Jews' 119; on law 100; limitations of ideas 125; on objectivity 101; on superfluousness 99; on totalitarianism 98–9, 110
Aristotle 123
Ascetic Priest 55, 56
asceticism 55, 56
Auschwitz 33; gas chambers at, denial 67; Lyotard on 72, 74
autonomy 11, 69

Bacon, Francis 14
bad conscience 51, 52, 53, 55, 68, 71
Barbie, Klaus 67
Bauer, Bruno: on Christianity 7; on emancipation 1–11, 80; on Enlightenment 25; on Holocaust 25–6; on particularism of Jews 3–4, 5–7
Bauman, Zygmunt 14; and Adorno and Horkheimer 19–20, 23, 24; and Agamben 27; on antisemitism and nature 18–26, 27; Arendt contrasted 116; on Enlightenment 19–20
'Bayreuth idealism' 89n 90
Benjamin, Walter 38
biopolitics 27–31, 76, 78; subjectivity of 29
The Birth of Tragedy (Nietzsche) 85–7, 90, 91

Index   135

book, meaning of 42
Brahmanism 92
breach of contract, antisemitism as 50–60
Buddhism 92
burning bush, imagery 45

capitalism, monopoly 17, 19
Carpentras, desecration of cemetery at 67
causality 15, 16, 24, 30
choice, and antisemitism 61
Christianity 7, 10, 22; death of Christ 53, 54; as Jewish plot for world domination 94n
citizenship, granting of 28
civil rights (Rights of Man) 2, 5, 6, 9, 76
class, and antisemitism 61
classicism 98, 107
Cohen, Morris 19n
community, notion 11
concentration camps 109, 111, *see also* Auschwitz
concept, Jews as 18, 19; and Arendt 115; Bauman on 22, 24; and Manderson 46; and Sartre 60, *see also* Jewish people
conscience: bad 51, 52, 53, 55, 68, 71; meaning 53
consciousness 68, 69, 71
conspiracy theory 17
consumption, and aestheticization 40–5, 47
contradictions, internal 36–7
creativity, and destruction 30
Critical Legal Studies Conference, United Kingdom xviii
critical theory xvii, xviii, xix, xx; history 33; and Marx 1
cure 56

de Tocqueville, Alexis 113, 114
debt: absolute 54; and Ascetic Priest concept 55; to Jews 74; unpaid 53
Deleuze, Gilles 84n
Democrat 63, 64
denial of Holocaust 66–7
Derrida, Jacques 35, 44
destruction, and creativity 30
devaluation and revaluation 62
Dialectic of Enlightenment (Adorno and Horkheimer) xix, 13, 14, 18, 23
The Differend (Lyotard) 67

Dionysus 85, 86, 103, 106
domination: concept 23, 30; exchange-value 38–9; and knowledge 40; and nature 31–2; total 109–10
Dreyfus Affair 116, 117
Duhring, Eugen 50, 56, 57

emancipation: and Agamben 75, 76, 78, 79, 81; and antisemitism 67, 71, 81; and Arendt 121; and Bauer 1–11, 80; definition 68, 75; history 7; human 3; limits of xix; and Lyotard 68–9; and Nietzsche 52, 59, 60, 81; political 2–3, 4, 8, 11, 12
Enlightenment: Adorno and Horkheimer on 13, 14–18, 19–20; Bauman on 25; definition 14; and Holocaust 19; and nature 15; origins 15; superstition within 14–15
eternal antisemitism, theories xix, 113
ethics: legal *see* legal ethics; Lyotard on 66–75; *see also* morality
Ethnological Museum 106n
'exceptional Jews' 119
exchange-value 38–9, 52, 53
Exodus 45
extra-positivist basis for antisemitism 31

Farias, Victor 67
fatalism 26–7
Faurisson, Robert 67
Feuerbach, Ludwig 7
formalism 37
France: Dreyfus Affair 116, 117; Prussia, defeat of (1807) 118; scandals in 66–7
function of antisemitism 17

garden, imagery of 23–4
gas chambers, denial 66–7
GBI (SS front) 105
genealogy: Arendt's thinking on antisemitism as 116; meaning 84; of morality 50–1, 53, 56; of the noble *see* *The Birth of Tragedy*; *On the Genealogy of Morals*
Goebbels, Joseph 104
'good and bad'/'good and evil' 88, 91, 93, 99
Greek classicism 98
Grundnorm 44, 45
guilt 53, 54, 120

Hampton Court, gardens at 23
Hart, HLA 34, 37, 38, 47
Hegel, Georg Wilhelm 33, 37
'Heidegger Affair' 67
Heidegger and 'the Jews' (Lyotard) 67
Hitler, Adolf 103
Holocaust, and monopoly capitalism 19
Holocaust dissolution 50
homo sacer (scared man) 29n 78
Horkheimer, Max: and Bauman 19–20, 23, 24; on causality 15, 16, 24, 30; and concentration camps 111; on Enlightenment 13, 14–18, 19–20; on Holocaust 19; on knowledge and domination 40; and Nazism 100; social theory 110
human emancipation 3
humanity, superfluousness of 102
hunger, love distinguished 40, 45

imminent critique 34–9, 47; absolute 38–9; internal contradictions 36–7; utopian negativity 37–8, 39
injustice, and legal positivism 35
inscription 28
integration 31
internal contradictions 36–7
irony 84–5

Jameson, Frederic 13n
Jarvis, Simon 36, 38
Jaskot, Paul B 105, 111
Jephcott, Edmund 13n
Jewish people: as anachronism, alleged 7; 'authentic', Nazi concept 30; as concept *see* concept, Jews as; as 'distortion' or 'effigy' 64–5, 73; 'exceptional' 119; Judaism without Jews 45–7; Marx on 7–8; and money/finance 8–10; negative status 21; as 'Other' 70; particularism, alleged 3–4, 5–7; Sartre on 64–5; as social pariahs 118
'Jewish type' 119–20
'Jewishness', as racial characteristic 120, 121
Judaism: and Christianity 10; and legal ethics 45, 46; 'materialist' basis 10; post-Holocaust notion of 45; 'without Jews' 45–7
jude bonus xviii
justice, and revenge 57–8

Kant, Immanuel 33
Kelsen, Hans 34, 37, 38, 44, 47
knowledge: and domination 40; of nature 28–29; scientific 27

Lanzmann, Claude 111
law: autonomy of 37; contradictions within concept 36–7; definitions 100; and subjectivity 101
Law for the Redesign of German Cities 104–5
legal ethics: and Judaism 45, 46; jurisdiction 41–4; jurisprudence 44–5; and positivism 34, 35, 36–7, 39
legal formalism 37
legal positivism: certainty of words 43; and legal ethics 36–7; Manderson on 34–5, 39, *see also* positivism
Levi, Primo 111
Levinas, Emmanuel 40, 45
logos, tragedy of 86, 95
loss, and *ressentiment see ressentiment*
love, hunger distinguished 40, 45
Lyotard, Jean-François xviii, 33, 49, 66–75; on consciousness 68, 69; on emancipation 68–9; on ethics 70; on Holocaust 74; on Nazism 77–8; and Nietzsche 68; on Other 70–1; on *ressentiment* 67, 73, 74, 81

Manderson, Desmond: on contradictions 36, 38; on ethics 34, 41–2, 44; on hunger and love 40, 45; on legal positivism 39, 41; on ownership 42
market capitalism 17
Marx, Karl xx, 1–12, 37; on Bauer 1–4, 5; on civil rights (Rights of Man) 2, 5, 6, 9; on money and finance 8–9; on political rights (Rights of the Citizen) 2, 3, 63; on private property 3, 6; and Sartre 60; on state 3–5
Minima Moralia (Adorno) 84–5
Mishnah 43, 45
Modernity and the Holocaust (Bauman) 14
money and finance 8–10
monopoly capitalism, transfer from market economy 17, 19
monumental architecture, Nazi 97–112; aesthetics 107; and concentration camps 109, 111; as parody of

classicism 106; as propaganda 103–4; and *ressentiment* 99; style 97–8, 108, *see also* Nazism
morality: genealogy of 50–1, 53, 56; good and evil 88; slave 61; and social life 52
Musselman 77, 78, 79–80
myth, demise of 86

nation: concept 27–8; inauthentic 65
National Socialism 67
natural science 15, 20–1, 22
nature/natural laws 14; and antisemitism, Bauman on 18–26, 27; humanity 15; Nazi Law of Nature as parody of 106, 100–3; and non-natural basis for antisemitism 31; and political power 28–9; and positivism 15, 16, 18, 29; social nature 16, 20
Nazism: Agamben on 29–30, 31, 77–8; deprivation of Jewish rights 123; diaries 104n; Jewish people, creation and destruction 30; Lyotard on 77–8; monumental architecture 97–112; nature, law of 102, 103; racist totalitarianism of 37; self-image 98; slavery, parody of 108–11; superfluousness 101; totalitarianism 37, 104, 105, 106, *see also* National Socialism; Third Reich
Negative Dialectics (Adorno) 33
Nietzsche, Friedrich 11, 49; anti-asceticism 92; anti–clericalism 92; on antisemitism as breach of contract 50–60; Arendt contrasted 116; on Ascetic Priest 55, 56; on bad conscience 52, 53, 55, 68, 71; on emancipation 52, 59, 60, 81; on genealogy of morality 50–1, 53, 56; and Lyotard 68; on *ressentiment* 51, 53, 54, 55, 56–9, 63, 65, 67, 73, 92; and Sartre 65–6; on 'Sovereign Individuals' 51, 55; on Wagner 85, 87, 89–91; on will to power 52, 88, *see also On the Genealogy of Morals* (Nietzsche); *The Birth of Tragedy* (Nietzsche)
noble: concept 88; demise of 89; genealogy of *see The Birth of Tragedy*; *On the Genealogy of Morals*; rebirth of 87; subjectivity 88–9

objectivity 101
Old Testament 74

On the Genealogy of Morals (Nietzsche) 50; and genealogy of noble 88–95; as a polemic 84–5; section 7 83–5, 89, 91, 92, 95
On the Jewish Question (Marx) xx, 1–2, 60
On Violence (Arendt) 13
origins of antisemitism, Arendt on 98–9, 121, 125
Other, the 70–1
ownership 42

paradigms 26, 30, 31, 32, 78; Holocaust as 77
parent-child relationship 42
parody 98, 99, 106; laws of nature 100–3; of slavery 108–11
Parsifal, critique of 90
particularism, Jewish 3–4, 5–7
Passover 45
'petrified values', of antisemite 65
political emancipation 2–3, 4, 8, 11, 12
political realm, equality 123–24
political rights (Rights of the Citizen) 2, 3, 63, 76
positivism 14, 30, 40–1; dominatory and authoritarian tendencies 36; imminent critique 34–9; and legal ethics 34, 35; and nature/naturalism 15, 16, 18, 29; of power 23; text 43, *see also* legal positivism; science, natural
power, and antisemitism 19, 23
Priests 89; Ascetic Priest 55, 56
primitive possession 61
private property: Marx on 3, 6, 9–10; Sartre on 61–2
private realm, and political realm 123, 124
psychoanalysis 68

racist antisemitism 21, 22, 27
religion, emancipation of state from 3
religious freedoms, Rights of Man 6
Remnants of Auschwitz (Agamben) 27, 77
ressentiment xviii, xx, 49, 50, 80; and Agamben 75, 76, 79, 80, 81; and Goebbels 104; and Lyotard 67, 72–3, 74, 81; and Marx 1, 11; and monumental architecture 99; and Nietzsche 51, 53, 54, 55, 56–9, 62, 65, 67, 73, 92; and parody 98, 99; and

Sartre 60, 61, 62, 63, 64, 67, 73; and slavery, parody of 108
restricted nature of Jews, alleged 3–4, 5–7
revenge 57–8
Rights of the Citizen 2, 3, 63, 76
Rights of Man 2, 5, 6, 9, 76
Rome 98
roots of antisemitism, Arendt on 121, 125
Rose, Gillian 84–5

Safranski, Rudiger 90
Sartre, Jean-Paul 49, 60–6, 97; on Democrat 63, 64; on Holocaust 67; and Nietzsche 65–6; on primitive possession 61; and *ressentiment* 60, 61, 62, 63, 64, 67, 73
scapegoat thesis 80, 113
Schache, Wolfgang 106n–7n
science, natural 15, 20–1, 22
Scobie, Alex 98
Second Commandment 33–4
secularism 56
selection procedures 29
Sendak, Maurice 34, 39–40
slave morality 61, 68
slavery, parody of 108–11
social class, and antisemitism 61
social relations, and antisemitism 23, 24
Socrates 86–7, 89
Sovereign Individuals 51, 55
'species-being' 6
'species-life' 4
Speer, Albert 104
Spotts, Frederic 106, 107
state: Bauman on 19; Marx on 3–5
state-Jews 117

Steinberg, Elan 19n
Stephan, N 97
Stone, Alison 13n
subjectivity: of biopolitics 29; denial of as product of 99; human 16–17; and law 101; of noble 88–9; and *ressentiment* 65
suffering 52, 56, 58
superfluousness 99, 100, 102, 103, 123
superstition 14–15

Talmud 43, 45
Third Reich 76
Thompson, EP 49
Torah 45
totalitarianism: Arendt on 98–9, 110; Nazi 37, 104, 105, 106; and propaganda 104; racist 37

unconscious 68, 69, 72
use-value 38–9, 52
utopian negativity 37–8, 39

Versailles Palace, gardens at 23
victimisation theories 113
volk, myths of 37

Wagner, Richard 85, 87, 89–91
'weeds', Jewish people as 21
Where the Wild Things Are (Sendak) 34, 40, 43
will to power 52, 88
Wolters, R 97

Young Hegelians 1

zoë 27, 28